The Mind-Body Connection for Educators

The Mind-Body Connection for Educators

INTENTIONAL MOVEMENT

FOR WELLNESS

by Kathryn Kennedy, PhD

JB JOSSEY-BASS™

A Wiley Brand

Take time to listen to your inner child and their needs;
cultivate a safe space for them to heal, play, and create.
The freedom that results from doing so is profound and limitless.
With immense love and gratitude,
—Kathryn

CONTENTS

ABOUT THE AUTHOR

With one foot in digital and online learning and the other in mental health and wellness, Kathryn has been cultivating two primary passions for over 20 years. She serves as founder and principal consultant of Consult4Ed Group and founder and executive director of Wellness for Educators. On the digital and online learning side, Kathryn's past roles include director of the Michigan Virtual Learning Research Institute, the research arm of Michigan Virtual; director of Research for the International Association for K–12 Online Learning (iNACOL) (now the Aurora Institute); adjunct professor and advisor for the EdD program at the Johns Hopkins University School of Education; and assistant professor of instructional technology at Georgia Southern University. She is one of the founding editors-in-chief of both the *Journal of Online Learning Research* and the *Handbook of Research on K–12 Online and Blended Learning*. She currently serves on the Leadership Team for the National Standards for Quality Online Learning and engages in exciting work with her Consult4ED Group team, which consists of over 30 amazing consultants representing a variety of expertise in the education field. On the mental health and wellness side, Kathryn combined her work in education and wellness to create Wellness for Educators, a 501(c)(3) nonprofit that is invested in and passionate about supporting educators worldwide with research-based, trauma- and equity-informed trainings, coaching, and strategies for whole-school social, emotional, mental, and physical health and wellbeing. Her team at Wellness for Educators consists of inspirational educators, licensed mental health professionals, and certified somatic practitioners. She is also working on a memoir focused on her lived experience of and healing process from early childhood trauma. She resides in the Finger Lakes region of New York with her husband Curtis and their fur babies.

FOREWORD

Kathryn Kennedy is the rare person and author who successfully investigates her own challenges in a way that supports healing and thriving. Even more impressive is that she masterfully opens her exploration to others without ever sounding sanctimonious or minimizing the complexity of what educators are facing. She does this with empathy, humor, and intelligence and gives readers confidence that they, too, can invest in their own wellbeing and chart a joyful, easier path forward by attending to the mind-body connection.

As a therapist of over 20 years with more than a decade of experience in leadership roles at the intersection of education and mental health, I have a clear view of how difficult things are for educators and how much *The Mind-Body Connection for Educators* adds to the narrative and the solutions. When my co-authors and I wrote *WHOLE: What Teachers Need to Help Students Thrive* in 2019, we were sounding alarm bells about educator wellbeing. Fast-forward to the present day, and the stressors have amplified and escalated at a rate no one could have predicted just a few years ago.

If you are an educator and you find yourself in a perpetual survival state of fight, flight, or shutdown, you are in good company. Kathryn unpacks many of the policy and systemic issues that are causing so much stress with great care. But this book goes far beyond that macro lens by giving you practices and lifelines you can put in place immediately to invite yourself back into your own life and your own body. You deserve to take care of yourself. You deserve rest, connection, safety, joy, and the world's deepest appreciation for what you do every day.

Dive into this book and follow where your curiosity takes you. Try out the different practices and pay attention to what your nervous system wants more of – maybe it's practices that bring you energy or practices that help you feel calm. Whatever it is, this book and the Wellness for Educators community will give you a path to keep moving toward what you need to lighten the load. And Kathryn is a most sincere and perfect guide.

– Michelle Kinder, MEd., LPC, ACC

ACKNOWLEDGMENTS

"We work on ourselves in order to help others, but also we help others in order to work on ourselves."

— Pema Chödrön

This book is not only the story and foundation of Wellness for Educators, but it also serves as a small piece of my own journey. That journey wouldn't be what it is without those who have walked alongside me. As it's one of the practices listed in Chapter 8, I've created a gratitude list to acknowledge the multitude of support.

Gratitude to my family and friends – Thank you so much for your support!

Gratitude to Wiley and Jossey-Bass Publishers and my dedicated team – Ashante Thomas, Mary Beth Rosswurm, Pete Gaughan, Rahini Devi Radhakrishnan and Sunnye Collins. Thank you all for your guidance, patience, and support!

Gratitude to my pre-submission reviewers – Dr. Colin Ackerman, Dr. Cathy Cavanaugh, Dr. Méroudjie Denis, Dr. Wendy Drexler, Vickie Echols, Dr. Aileen Fullchange, Dr. Rebecca Itow, Dr. Curtis Jirsa, Liz Kennedy, Dr. J.J. Lewis, Margo Rosingana, Jonathan Santos Silva, Antonia Small, and Mary Snow. Thank you for taking the time to make this book so much better with your expertise and experience!

Gratitude for our Wellness for Educators' Board members, both past and present – Peter Arashiro, Dr. Mikela Bjork, Erika Bjorum, Dr. Carey Borkoski, Dr. Cathy Cavanaugh, Dr. Méroudjie Denis, Dystanie Douglas-Burger, Dr. Wendy Drexler, Dr. Tonia Dousay, Dr. Aileen Fullchange, Alejandra Ramos Gómez, Taylor Gonzalez, Dr. Nicol Howard, Dr. Rebecca Itow, Shomari Jones, Dr. J.J. Lewis, Dr. Tia Madkins, Brenda Maurao, Stephanie McGary, Judy Perez, Dr. Allison Powell, Meredith Roe, Francisco "Tito" Santos Silva, Jonathan Santos Silva. Sarika Simpson, Dr. Dacia Smith, Mark Sparvell, Sophie Teitlebaum, and Dr. Kristen Vogt. Thank you all for providing your expertise, guidance, and experience and for helping us navigate as we continue to grow.

Gratitude to our past and present staff, contractors, and partners – we are stronger together and can affect more change through meaningful collaboration!

Gratitude to my somatic psychology and mind-body education schools – Embody Lab and Transformative Programs – and teachers – Sheleana Aiyana, Bayo Akomolafe, Karine Bell, Micah Bizant, Kelsey Blackwell, Bonnie Bainbridge Cohen, Patrisse Cullors, Deb Dana, Lisa Dion, Lisa Jo Epstein, Mordecai Ettinger, Sam Field, Ruella Frank, Dr. Maureen Gallagher, Dr. Ruby Gibson, Dr. Sam Grant, Dr. Amber Elizabeth Gray, Dr. Angela Grayson, Staci Haines, Monica Hunken, Isaiah Jackson-Ramirez, Dr. Rae Johnson, Farzana Khan, Dr. Sará King, Rev. angel Kyodo williams, Zea Leguizamon, Dr. Peter Levine, Dr. Scott Lyons, Susan McConnell, Resmaa Menakem, Kekuni Minton, Manuela Mischke-Reeds, Sherri Mitchell, Rusia Mohiuddin, Jessica Montgovery, Emory Moore, Nikki Myers, Nkem Ndefo, Euphrasia Nyaki, Dr. Pat Ogden, Dr. Diane Poole Heller, Dr. Stephen Porges, Dr. Arielle Schwartz, Dr. Dan Siegel, Sam Taitel, Kai Cheng Thom, Dr. Bessel van der Kolk, and Dr. Albert Wong.

Gratitude to my yoga, meditation, mindfulness, and Qigong teachers – Aiyana Athenian, Ajeet, Mara Crans, Joan Hanley (Hari Kirin Kaur Khalsa), Snatam Kaur, Saibhung Kaur Khalsa, Sukhpran Kaur Khalsa, Balmeet Lasky, Mindy Miller Muse, Master Lisa O'Shea, Krishna Peter Perry, Satya Melissa Farr, Margo Rosingana, Prem Sadasivananda, Dr. Arielle Schwartz, Antonia Small, and Sagel Urlacher.

Gratitude to my somatic support systems – Heather Spangler (acupuncture), Sylvia Tavares (Emotional Freedom Technique), Anthony Fazio (acupuncture), and Paul Gagnon (massage therapy).

Gratitude to my therapists over the years – Dr. Jody Telfair-Richards, Dr. Nancy Coleman, Susan Miner, and Marissa Ahern.

Gratitude to Dr. Cathy Cavanaugh and Dr. Wendy Drexler for your friendship and mentorship, and for not only reviewing the book, but also for being part of Wellness for Educators' original board during our infancy. Thank you also for your support during my nervous breakdown. To know that I was not alone, especially in the academic journey, was so critically grounding during a very unstable time in my life.

Gratitude to my sisters – Liz Kennedy and Mary Snow – for your willingness to believe in the vision, for being creative ideation partners, and for graciously accepting delayed pay at the start of our journey (ha!). Thank you for being constants in my life – Love you!

Gratitude to my husband – Curtis – for being an amazing sounding board during my creative sparks and for supporting my need for Holy Donuts and other tasty treats during deadline dashes. Thank you for walking alongside me in the trauma-healing journey and life in general. Grateful to be present and walking alongside you in this life – Love you!

> "To be fully alive, fully human, and completely awake is to be continually thrown out of the nest. To live fully is to be always in no-man's-land, to experience each moment as completely new and fresh. To live is to be willing to die over and over again."
>
> – Pema Chödrön

Creating and expanding this organization and traveling on my trauma-healing journey continues to put me outside of my nest on a regular basis. I am grateful to myself for always choosing the path that is most meaningful to me, which has, more often than not, been the most challenging one.

"Usually we think that brave people have no fear. The truth is that they are intimate with fear."

– Pema Chödrön

Our journey of mental health and wellbeing is not a one and done. It's a daily practice. While it isn't always fun to do the work, if we approach it with compassionate curiosity, it can provide us with insight not only into our relationships with others, but most importantly, into our relationship with ourselves.

Gratitude to you for your willingness to care for yourself in whatever way is meaningful to you.

CHAPTER 1

My Path to Educator Wellness

Throughout this book, you will be invited to take an intentional pause. This will be a place where you can check in with yourself to see how your mind and body are feeling. You'll see the words *Intentional Pause* with the lotus image and a list of questions. This practice of intentionally pausing can help you build and strengthen your mind-body connection, and, when practiced regularly, heal trauma and prolonged stress.

INTENTIONAL PAUSE*

- ➤ What do I notice in my mind? (observe without judgment)
- ➤ What do I notice in my body? (observe without judgment)
- ➤ What do I notice in my feelings? (observe without judgment)
- ➤ What do I notice in my thoughts? (observe without judgment)
- ➤ What do I need at this moment to feel supported? (observe without judgment and give yourself what you need to feel supported)

*Note: Take an intentional pause whenever you feel like you need one, not just in the places where you are invited to do so.

I first started talking about my interest in educator wellbeing in 2017. Many of my friends and colleagues in the digital learning space were curious and confused, and rightfully so. Why would someone like me, a researcher in online and digital learning for almost two decades, want to delve into educator wellbeing?

From 2004 to 2018, I worked as a digital librarian and an instructional technology professor at a handful of universities, and as a director of research at a couple of nonprofit organizations. I'm a qualitative researcher, so over the years, I distributed questionnaires and surveys, conducted interviews and focus groups, collected and reviewed digital and analog artifacts – all in order to listen to, understand, and share educators' stories and lived experiences. I've heard from thousands of educators over time, including teachers, special education staff, English language learning specialists, school counselors, school psychologists, school librarians, educational technology coordinators, district administrators, school administrators, state policy makers, and more.

Even though the research projects I've worked on and continue to work on are mostly focused on online and digital learning, the main theme across all of them has been educator stress (including secondary traumatic stress), trauma, and burnout. Anyone close to or involved directly in the field of education knows that educators have been pushed to the limits by constant change; intense focus on high-stakes, standards-based teaching; initiative fatigue; among many other stressors. Hearing these stories again and again as an educator myself was really hard to handle without doing something about it. Additionally and simultaneously, since 1985, I have been on a personal journey to understand and support my own mental health and wellbeing.

MY MENTAL HEALTH JOURNEY

I was six years old when my father tried to kill my mother. I was in the room with them when it happened. I didn't know it at the time, but this was my father's second attempt at trying to hurt my mother. Because he was a Korean War veteran, my father was hospitalized at the Bedford VA Hospital in Massachusetts. The health professionals diagnosed him with bipolar disorder. The hospital and my family encouraged him to get the help he needed, which included medication and a regular therapy schedule. He didn't want anything to do with that, and instead of staying near the hospital and our family for the support we all needed, he wanted to escape from the pressure.

That escape came in 1987 when my father decided to move us to Florida. No one except my father wanted it to happen. No one could stop him either. On the day we were leaving for Florida, everyone gathered at our house in Medford, where my parents had lived for over 30 years. The camper was packed, and when we started to pull away, I ran to the back window, waving frantically and crying uncontrollably, while those who could keep me safe grew smaller and smaller.

Like all the other times we traveled in our camper, I laid in the top bunk above the driver's cabin and counted the lines on the highway as we trekked south to the Sunshine State. After four nights at campgrounds along the way, we arrived at Fort Myers Beach, where we lived in our camper for the summer. Right before school started, my parents found a house in Cape Coral and enrolled me in 4th grade.

On my first day of school, my teacher introduced herself and laid out the ground rules of her classroom. She had an apple tree made of construction paper on the back wall of the classroom. Each student's name was assigned to an apple. Our teacher explained that if you didn't do your homework, if you were late to school, or if you did something wrong, you would have to put a worm in your apple. To do this, you would go to the front of the classroom, get a worm from the teacher, and walk to the back of the room to put the worm in your apple. By the end of the week, if you had five or more worms in your apple, you didn't go to recess.

Given what I had been through and what I was still going through, I rebelled by not completing my schoolwork, and by being oppositional and exhibiting what adults thought of as "bad behavior." Consequently, I had the most worms in my apple every week and didn't participate in recess at all that year. Even though I was hell-bent on causing as many problems as I could at school, I advanced to 5th grade.

This is when I met Mr. Weaver, the educator who had the biggest impact on my life. Even on the first day of school, I knew things would be different. Mr. Weaver sat us down and took the time to get to know each of us. He took the time to establish meaningful relationships with us and make the learning environment safe and inclusive. He encouraged healthy collaboration with others. He got to know the "why" behind our behaviors and the "how" and "what" we needed to feel supported. I'm grateful each day I think back on Mr. Weaver. Things could have gone much differently for me had we not crossed paths. I never missed a day of recess that year, and I improved academically.

Fast-forward to 1992. I was 14. My dad tried to hurt my mom again. I was in the room with them when it happened. The next day, without my dad knowing, my mom and I flew to Boston to live with family. My mom almost went through with a divorce, but within three months, despite my family's objections and my dad's continued refusal to get help to support himself, my mom and I moved back to Florida to live with him again.

For a long time, one of the questions I reflected on in therapy was what did it feel like to live in a space that was not safe, especially as a child? My brain did its job to suppress what happened when I was six since I didn't have the capacity to process it at that time. Despite that, my body and mind remembered the trauma. I experienced recurring nightmares and anxiety into my teenage years because I didn't express and work through my emotions and experiences (and really didn't know how to at the time). I engaged with counselors and therapists, including an art therapist who helped me get rid of my recurring nightmare. I used cognitive behavioral therapy to shift the challenging feelings and emotions brought on by trauma and prolonged stress. Though the cognitive-based therapy helped me work through my understanding of my experiences, I was still not 100%.

The toll that trauma had taken on me resurfaced in 2009 when I was 30. I was in the middle of my doctoral program at the University of Florida. At the time, I was working on my dissertation focused on the importance of teaching teachers how to teach online. I was conducting three research studies alongside one of my doctoral advisors. I was teaching two undergraduate courses to preservice teachers. I was enrolled in three graduate courses. I was serving as a supervisor teacher for six masters-level preservice teachers who were interested in learning what it's like to teach in an online school. I was working a part-time job in order to put myself through school. At that time, I had multiple loans I was paying back so they wouldn't incur interest. I was in an unhealthy long-distance relationship. Long story short, I was under a lot of pressure and stress.

Around that time, I found out one of my family members tried to commit suicide, and they didn't want me to tell anyone else. My mom, who was 75 at the time, came to visit me in Florida for the winter, and while she was with me, she fell down the stairs at my apartment complex and suffered a hematoma and severe concussion. She was okay, thank goodness.

Once I knew my mom was okay, I suffered a nervous breakdown and was admitted to the hospital. I started having frequent panic attacks, which I had never had before. After being pushed to take medication that caused me to have suicidal thoughts, I started seeing a university counselor who told me to "put on my big girl panties" and keep taking the meds. I listened because I honestly didn't know what else to do at that point. But after having a scary experience where I woke up at 3 a.m. on the bottom of my tub with the shower head pouring down on me and the water up to my nose, I decided to take a three-month leave of absence from my doctoral program and moved to Maine to live with my family.

During that time, I couldn't do anything. My mind just wasn't functioning the way it used to, and I was really scared. I was experiencing acute agoraphobia (fear of going out and being in public) because I was afraid of having panic attacks in public. With the support and safety of my family and friends, and after many months of a combination of cognitive behavioral therapy (CBT), Emotional Freedom Technique (EFT), Eye Movement Desensitization and Reprocessing (EMDR), yoga, group exercise, and meditation, I was able to resume my doctoral program and graduated that year.

In 2010, I was so curious about my inability to learn when I was extremely stressed and traumatized that I set off on a learning journey through thousands of hours of training in neuroscience, somatic psychology, embodiment, trauma healing, yoga, mindfulness, meditation, Qigong, and more. We'll dive into what I learned while on my journey in the next chapter, "The Intersection of Mental Health, Wellbeing, and Learning."

In 2018, after 18 years of working in multiple nonprofits, I took a leap of faith into the world of education consulting to continue my work in the area of online and digital learning. On New Year's Eve that year, I was excited to see what 2019 had in store for me. I tossed and turned all night with an overwhelming need to merge my passions for education, mental health, and wellbeing, and create much-needed support for educators. This sleepless night led to the birth of Wellness for Educators.

INTENTIONAL PAUSE

- ➤ What do I notice in my mind? (observe without judgment)
- ➤ What do I notice in my body? (observe without judgment)
- ➤ What do I notice in my feelings? (observe without judgment)
- ➤ What do I notice in my thoughts? (observe without judgment)
- ➤ What do I need at this moment to feel supported? (observe without judgment and give yourself what you need to feel supported)

THE BIRTH OF WELLNESS FOR EDUCATORS

After noodling on the idea of Wellness for Educators, I shared it with my two older sisters, Mary and Liz, both of whom have ties to education and mental health and wellbeing. Mary started her teaching career in mid-coast Maine after graduating from Lesley College (now Lesley University) in 1980. For 36 years, she served in a variety of teaching roles including special education for K–8, general education for K–4, and substance abuse counseling for K–12. Liz also attended Lesley University and graduated in 1995 with her Bachelor of Science degree in Natural Science and Certificate in Early Childhood Education. She served in administration and management in the healthcare field for over 25 years. Both offered feedback as I iterated on ideas for what we could do with the organization. Based on their feedback, we started small on a shoe-string budget.

Figure 1.1 Sisters from left to right – Kathryn Kennedy, Mary Snow, and Liz Kennedy.

We worked with a friend of Mary's who is a local author and illustrator – Mary Beth Owens – to design our first logo.

Figure 1.2 Original logo.

We also created a small digital Wellness Library. The vision for the library was based on the idea that educators don't have much time throughout the day, but, as research shows, even short mind-body practices can help support our nervous system, and heal trauma and prolonged stress.

By the end of the year, we created a website that housed our Wellness Library, a collection of over 100 videos, pictures, audio files, and transcripts focused on yoga, meditation, breathwork, Qigong, and mindfulness. We intentionally made this library free because we wanted to give everyone access. The pictures that illustrate the practices in Chapters 5–10 are the ones that we use in the library.

Visit the Wellness for Educators' Wellness Library at well4edu.org/wellness-library

---

At the same time as we were creating the Wellness Library, I was offering yoga and meditation sessions at the conferences I was attending for my work in digital learning. Since I enjoyed hearing educator stories, I also started a podcast where educators could share their wellness journeys. We hosted webinars with panels of educators who explored different topics related to educator wellness. We also held a few book studies.

As we continued to add more and more offerings, we invited a group of advisors to serve as a sounding board for our ideas. By the end of 2019, we were still grappling with what to do next with Wellness for Educators. At that time, the organization was an assumed name under my education consulting firm. I felt like we needed to do more, and I was throwing around the idea of shifting the organization to a 501(c)(3) nonprofit, but had neither the time nor the resources to do it.

In late February 2020, Liz and I attended the Digital Learning Annual Conference (DLAC). At DLAC, we did a soft launch of Wellness for Educators. It was the first time we shared what we were doing with a larger audience outside of our small social media following. We received feedback from conference attendees about what we could do programmatically to support educators. We flew back home to Portland, Maine, on February 27, 2020, excited to see what we could do with all the feedback we received. Then, the COVID-19 pandemic hit.

COVID-INFLUENCED EXPANSION

Given my background in teaching teachers how to teach online and creating engaging online and blended learning environments, my education consulting work exploded at the start of the pandemic. I was pulled into several large digital learning consulting contracts focused on advising states, schools, districts, nonprofit organizations, and companies on how they could make a quick shift from traditional learning to online learning. At the same time, I was extremely worried about the wellbeing of the field.

The education system was in complete and utter chaos. Educators were shifting to an unknown teaching and learning practice. School leaders had to shift their practices to lead in remote and online learning environments and support their communities in making that shift as well. Parents, caregivers, and families took on additional responsibilities in supporting their students' learning. Students were thrown into a learning environment that they were not ready to learn in. There was a lot of change and lack of safety and meaningful connection. No one was prepared to do what they needed to, and everyone went into overdrive in order to "keep up" during a global pandemic.

Educators, schools, and districts were constantly being critiqued while doing something they weren't prepared to do. As everyone started to come back to their physical schools, some educators had to sign over their lives saying that they wouldn't hold their school liable if they got sick or died of COVID. There was so much instability with the constant shift in and out of schools as they experienced outbreaks and temporary quarantines. The field started focusing on learning loss and learning gaps, causing feelings of shame and guilt for educators, parents, caregivers, families, communities, and students, who were all doing their best in the middle of an absolutely crazy time in our history.

Educators were wearing more hats than they should have been (as usual). They were being asked to provide mental health and wellbeing, and social and emotional learning supports to their students and families, as well as serve as technology assistants for parents, caregivers, families, students, and colleagues when the majority of educators were barely trained or prepared for any of it. In addition to that, they were also trying to take care of themselves and their own families in the middle of a global pandemic. The field of education went into overdrive with no room for any of its stakeholders to take care of themselves. Watching the pressure put on educators, students, and caregivers was extremely overwhelming, saddening, and frustrating. The stress and trauma felt and experienced by educators is unfortunately disproportionately higher for communities of color, for women, and for those identifying as LGBTQIA+, especially in the current political climate.

The tipping point that ultimately led me to shift Wellness for Educators to a 501(c)(3) nonprofit happened in fall of 2020. I was involved in multiple consulting projects focused on digital learning. I urged clients at that time to include mental health and wellbeing support in their products and programming. Some said "yes" while others felt it was overkill and unnecessary. Some included supports only for social emotional learning (SEL). *SEL* is often used interchangeably with *mental health* and *wellbeing*. SEL is an important part of the overarching topic of mental health and wellbeing, but I didn't feel like it was enough. I conveyed this to my clients, emphasizing that, given the amount of prolonged stress and trauma educators were experiencing, educators would start leaving the field if they didn't feel mentally well, heard, and supported. And, as we know from research, whether they stay in the field or not, if educators and their nervous systems are not supported, their overwhelm, in whatever form it takes, will transfer to others in their community, including students, colleagues, and parents/caregivers.

That experience catalyzed me. Despite our lack of capacity, in December 2020, we started to increase what we were doing and shifted the organization out of my education consulting firm and established it as a stand-alone 501(c)(3) nonprofit. Our first full year as a nonprofit was 2021. We've continued to expand our work ever since.

SWIM

No doubt, educators have been in a state of prolonged stress and trauma. Only in 2022, two years after the start of the pandemic, did I start to hear some of the field acknowledging that what had happened – and what is continuing to happen – was traumatic and stressful for educators, students, and caregivers, and the world at large. Throughout the pandemic, educators at their boiling point were not okay and were ready to look for exits out of the field despite their love for it. Educators are still suffering from the trauma of teaching and leading during the pandemic.

If you're an educator, you know that change takes time. Despite everything that has happened in the field, there are pockets of hope when it comes to the system making a shift to better support educators. More and more schools and districts are taking steps to invest in educator wellness. In the work we are doing, we emphasize that educator wellness is not an individual effort; rather, it is a system-level effort. As one of my teachers, Dr. Albert Wong, a somatic psychotherapist, said during one of my certificate programs, "Challenges within communities or systems need interventions at the level of communities or systems."

Grounded in three research-based, trauma- and equity-informed models,[1] we created S.W.I.M., System-wide Wellness Implementation Model. Informed by somatic psychology, this model intentionally aligns mind-body connection education and practices for every stakeholder, including leaders, educators, students, and families/caregivers. The model's implementation supports systems to cultivate safe, culturally responsive, community-centric, humanity-driven learning spaces, similar to the one I experienced in Mr. Weaver's 5th-grade classroom.

Figure 1.3 System-Wide Wellness Implementation Model (SWIM) logo.

Mental health and wellbeing are at the center of this model and led us to contract licensed mental health professionals, including clinical social workers, master social workers, psychologists, therapists, and counselors, as well as educators in the field who were advocates of mental health and wellbeing in their work. Our team also expanded to include certified somatic professionals who support mind-body healing modalities, including but not limited to yoga, meditation, Qigong, art, music, and dance. The foundation of what we do at Wellness for Educators is to provide mind-body connection education and practices to heal prolonged stress and trauma.

So why write this book and the other three that will follow in this series? During our programming, we don't always have the opportunity to share the "why" behind what we do. Our "why" is couched in the science behind the mind-body connection education and practices that support mental health and wellbeing. The book series provides a deeper dive into our "why" and a closer look at many of the practices and strategies we use in our practices-based programming. We believe the series will offer educators a window of opportunity to support their individual mental health and wellbeing, and serve as a resource for teams of educators implementing a vision of cultivating and sustaining whole-district and school culture, and mental health and wellbeing.

My initial motivation to learn more about my experiences with trauma and prolonged stress centered on my fear of not knowing what was happening to me when I was struggling. I also looked at continuing to learn as a way to take back my power, which is often lost when we experience trauma. As I learned more and as my self-compassion and experiences grew, that fear eventually shifted into empowerment, insatiable curiosity, unrelenting motivation, and intrigued interest in gaining more knowledge. That fervor for learning formed the foundation of our work at Wellness for Educators, which thrives at the intersection of mental health, trauma, prolonged stress, healing, and its effect on our ability to teach, lead, and learn.

Figure 1.4 Intersection of mental health, wellbeing, and learning.

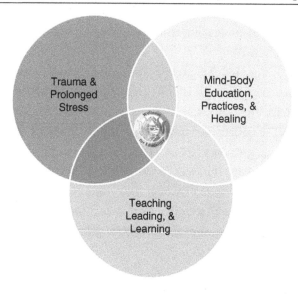

HOW TO USE THIS BOOK

This book is informally divided into two sections. The first section consists of Chapters 1 through 4, which provide the foundational information and research for the importance of why the mind-body connection is so vitally important for educators. One of the chapters acknowledges the school- and systemic-level issues that often get in the way of educator wellness. This section also includes the research and models that focus on educator wellness at the individual, system and community levels.

The second section includes Chapters 5 through 10. This section provides an overview of five disciplines that align with the subtitle of the current book in this series: "Intentional Movement for Wellness," including yoga, breathwork, meditation, mindfulness, Qigong, and yin yoga.

The book concludes with a wicked short yet poignant Chapter 11 that focuses on next steps and provides a sneak peek of the second, third, and fourth books in this series.

This book was not really designed to read straight through, though you're welcome to do that if it works best for you. To begin, I suggest reading the first four chapters to provide yourself with a foundation for understanding the *why* behind mind-body connection. These chapters serve as a useful building block to also understanding the importance of intentional movement for mind-body connection, the strategies of which are shared in Chapters 5 through 10.

Once you've digested Chapters 1 through 4, read each of the strategy chapters (Chapters 5 through 10) on their own over a longer period of time so that you have the opportunity and space to intentionally incorporate and reflect on the concepts, which can be pretty dense for those new to a practice, and strategies for yourself as well as with your colleagues and students. For those of you who may be familiar with one or more of the practices, perhaps you could read through those initially and then dig deeper into the other practices that you're not as familiar with. You might also gravitate to one practice more than another. Be open to whichever resonates most with you.

As I reiterate in Chapter 11, I was driven to write this book and share it with the field of education at large because of the meaningful impact these concepts, practices, and strategies have had on my life, both personally and professionally. While this book is focused on an action plan for educators personally, I encourage you to share this book with others in your school and district. Introduce the book to your wellness committees, and if you don't have a committee, be the agent of change for your school and/or district to establish and implement one. Taking action at the personal level is so important, and then being the lighthouse for others around you, including colleagues, students, parents, caregivers, and community, is vital for infusing humanity in our education systems.

Additionally, given the title, this book is very clearly written for educators, but the majority of its content is applicable to anyone wishing to learn more about healing trauma. The more we know and share about these concepts, practices, and strategies, the more we can center humanity in our world at large.

INTENTIONAL PAUSE

➤ What do I notice in my mind? (observe without judgment)
➤ What do I notice in my body? (observe without judgment)
➤ What do I notice in my feelings? (observe without judgment)
➤ What do I notice in my thoughts? (observe without judgment)
➤ What do I need at this moment to feel supported? (observe without judgment and give yourself what you need to feel supported)

You might be asking: *Why is this mind-body connection so vitally important to the field of education*? Let's explore that!

NOTE

1. (1) Organisation for Economic Co-operation and Development's Teacher Wellbeing Framework; (2) Collaboration for Academic, Social, and Emotional Learning (CASEL's) Schoolwide Indicators; and (3) Centers for Disease Control and Prevention and the Association for Supervision and Curriculum Development's (ASCD) Whole School, Whole Community, Whole Child (WSCC) Model.

CHAPTER 2

The Intersection of Mental Health, Wellbeing, and Learning

As is mentioned in Chapter 1, I was curious about why my mind and body completely shut down during my nervous breakdown, and I wanted to understand why that was. So, in 2010, I began my journey into the fields of neuroscience, somatic psychology, embodiment, developmental psychopathology, interpersonal neurobiology, and more. I was also continuing to see different mind-body practitioners (Emotional Freedom Technique, Qigong, yoga, meditation). Each time I saw a practitioner, something would change in me, and I would feel better. I would then harness my inner researcher, who I like to call my inner toddler, and ask the practitioner for more information and explain to me *Why?* Admittedly, I had more questions than answers.

Why did that particular strategy work?
Why did my nightmares stop?
Why did my anxiety diminish?
Why did my panic attacks go away?
Why did I start to feel better?
Why did my relationships improve with others?
Why did my relationship with myself improve?
Why did my ability to learn come back?
Why did it take me three months or more to start to feel like myself again?

After soaking in the knowledge from my own self-study and the additional resources that my therapists and mind-body practitioners provided me, everything started to slowly click into place.

All my whys resulted and continue to result in one common theme that centered on the connection between the mind and the body. We often talk about the mind and body as two separate entities, but research shows otherwise – our mind and body are inextricably linked, especially when it comes to our experiences with prolonged stress and trauma. Before we jump into the rest of this chapter, I want to take a minute to define *trauma*, a common phenomenon that is, unfortunately, often misunderstood.

DEFINING *TRAUMA*

When everything was happening in my life, I didn't know that what I was experiencing was traumatic nor did I really know what trauma was. Over the years, and still today, I talk to many people who believe trauma is only experienced by those who serve and fight in a war. As I've learned over time, this is not the case.

> *Trauma* can be any stress that overwhelms our body's and/or our brain's ability to cope.

Here is a list of examples of trauma:

- Natural disasters and their aftereffects
- Chronic experiences (child abuse, neglect)
- War, combat, refugee camps, concentration camps
- Major surgeries
- Life-threatening illnesses
- Serious injury
- Serious accidents
- Rape or sexual assault
- Mass disasters – terror attacks, school shootings

- Torture or kidnapping
- Physical abuse
- Sexual abuse
- Emotional abuse
- Physical neglect
- Emotional neglect
- Mental illness
- Incarceration
- Family members or friends treated violently
- Family member who is experiencing addiction
- Verbal abuse
- Losing someone to separation, divorce, or death

Note that this list is not an exhaustive list, and there is an important reason for that. Because traumatic experiences are those that put us outside of our ability to cope, trauma is very subjective; responses to an experience can vary from one person to another. Also, trauma can be collective and compounding, meaning there can be multiple traumatic experiences happening at one time in our lives. For many, for instance, the pandemic has been (and continues to be for some) an underlying source of prolonged stress, and any additional stress layered onto that has the potential to cause trauma.

In addition to direct experiences with trauma, we can experience vicarious trauma when we are serving as support or witness to someone else's trauma. This phenomenon is known as vicarious trauma or secondary traumatic stress. So even if we are not experiencing something directly, we can still feel the effects of what that person is experiencing. This is something we as educators experience on a daily basis.

Additionally, trauma doesn't have to be one extreme event. For example, one of my teachers, Nkem Ndefo, MSN, CNM, RN, shared her thoughts during one of our trainings about how Western society and continuous racist, sexist, transphobic (all the -ists, -ics, and -isms) acts (even when they do not happen to us personally) are traumatic, especially for women, people of color, and those who identify as LGBTQIA+:

> We think of trauma as things like rape, robbery, and car accidents. But there's also the slow grind of systems of multiple oppressions, the slow grind of microaggressions and macroaggressions, the constant emphasis on production and working and never resting. That overwhelming trauma is the norm in North American culture.

Building on this idea of prolonged stress and trauma, another one of my teachers, Dr. Arielle Schwartz, a licensed clinical psychologist, shared during one of our trainings that, when not worked through, prolonged stress and trauma can settle into our body and mind as post-traumatic stress disorder (PTSD). Over the years, I've had the pleasure of hearing Dr. Peter Levine, author of *Waking the Tiger: Healing Trauma*, speak in my training programs. One of his well-known quotes really resonates with me, especially after what I've experienced in my own life and what I've unfortunately witnessed in the field of education and the world at large during the pandemic: "Trauma is perhaps the most avoided, ignored, belittled, denied, misunderstood, and untreated cause of human suffering." Even though everything seems to be going back to "normal" in the field of education, I think we've only just begun to see the effects of trauma and prolonged stress. Because some in the field will choose to continue to ignore its presence and not take the time to thoroughly heal, the effects of trauma and prolonged stress will continue to resurface as time goes on. Levine explains:

> Trauma has become so commonplace that most people don't even recognize its presence. It affects everyone. Each of us has had a traumatic experience at some point in our lives, regardless of whether it left us with an obvious case of post-traumatic stress. . . . Because trauma symptoms can remain hidden for years after a triggering event, some of us who have been traumatized are not yet symptomatic. . . . (p. 41) In our culture there is a lack of tolerance for the emotional vulnerability that traumatized people experience. Little time is allotted for the

working through of emotional events. We are routinely pressured into adjusting too quickly in the aftermath of an overwhelming situation. Denial is so common in our culture that it has become a cliché. (1997, p. 48)

In the next several sections of this chapter, we'll delve a bit deeper into understanding trauma and prolonged stress by exploring the Adverse Childhood Experiences (ACEs) Study, the Polyvagal Theory, the Window of Tolerance, and the brain and learning. These theories and frameworks are important to understand because they undergird the SWIM model.

THE ACEs STUDY

One of the major developments in research that brought attention and validity to the mind-body connection was the Adverse Childhood Experiences (ACEs) Study. Between 1995 and 1997, the ACEs Study was conducted by a team of doctors from the Centers for Disease Control and Prevention (CDC) and Kaiser Permanente. The full results can be found in the May 1998 issue of the *American Journal of Preventive Medicine* (Felitti et al. 1998); this chapter shares key components and learnings from the study.

The ACEs Study distributed a questionnaire to over 17,000 participants, asking them about their experiences with the following adverse childhood experiences:

- Physical abuse
- Sexual abuse
- Emotional abuse
- Physical neglect
- Emotional neglect
- Mental illness
- Divorce
- Substance abuse

- Violence against mother
- Having a relative who has been sent to jail or prison

In the study itself, these categories were collapsed into a total of seven choices, including:

1. Psychological abuse
2. Physical abuse
3. Sexual abuse
4. Violence against mother
5. Living with household members who were substance abusers
6. Living with household members who were mentally ill (including suicidal)
7. Living with household members who were imprisoned

It's important to note that the ACEs do not have to happen directly to a child to be counted; ACEs can also be counted if a child has witnessed the experiences happening to another person. This is known as vicarious trauma or secondary traumatic stress, which can lead to compassion fatigue. These terms are more often associated with educators and those in the helping fields, but it is important for us as educators to understand that children and adolescents can also experience vicarious trauma, secondary traumatic stress, and compassion fatigue.

The results of the study showed that over half of the respondents had at least one of the seven ACEs, while one-fourth of the respondents reported having experienced two or more. Based on the study's analysis, the researchers found a dose-response relationship between the number of ACEs a person reported, and that person's behaviors and diseases in their adult life. What does *dose-response relationship* mean? This means that the higher the number of ACEs a person has experienced, the greater the risk to their health later in life. As an example, in the study, if a person experienced four or more ACEs, they were twice as likely to develop heart disease and cancer as adults. According to Dr. Vincent Felitti, director of the ACEs Study, "contrary to conventional belief, time does not heal all wounds since humans convert traumatic and stressful emotional experiences into organic disease." The ACEs Study also shows that these experiences are more prevalent for certain populations, including those who have low income and education, people of color, and people who identify as LGBTQIA+.

The ACEs Study was also noted in Dr. Bessel van der Kolk's book titled *The Body Keeps the Score: Brain, Mind, and Body in the Healing of Trauma.* This is one of the books that is foundational to our work at Wellness for Educators. Co-founder of the Trauma Research Foundation, van der Kolk has studied trauma recovery and healing since the early 1970s. In his book, van der Kolk covers the scientific explanation of how trauma is not only stored in our minds, but also in our bodies. Because of that, van der Kolk emphasizes that mind-based therapies alone, such as cognitive behavioral therapy or talk therapy, cannot be the sole method for those recovering from trauma and prolonged stress. In addition to mind-based therapies, mind-body education and practices, such as the ones shared in this book among many others, are also needed. Mind-body education and practices can free up the residue left behind in the body by unhealed trauma and prolonged stress.

With a personal ACE score of seven, the study findings align with my own lived experience. I engaged in cognitive behavioral therapy for many years, and while it was helpful, it wasn't until I learned more about the mind-body connection through my own self-study and participated in mind-body practices that I was able to heal what was happening inside of me. Unfortunately, it took a while for me to get to that point. Before that, I engaged in addictive behaviors that weren't healthy, such as workaholism. As I would later learn from Dr. Gabor Maté, author of *In the Realm of Hungry Ghosts: Close Encounters with Addiction*, that addiction and other conditions, such as attention deficit disorder (ADD) and attention deficit/hyperactivity disorder (ADHD) (for Maté's work on ADD and ADHD, see *Scattered Minds: The Origins and Healing of Attention Deficit Disorder*) stem from unresolved trauma.

Because of my workaholism, I wore out my thyroid. First, I had hyper-thyroidism, which then progressed into hypothyroidism. Soon after my nervous breakdown, when I was on my path to recovering, I found out that my hypothyroidism had advanced into an autoimmune disorder called Hashimoto's thyroiditis, a condition where your body doesn't recognize your thyroid and starts attacking it. Working with a naturopathic doctor, I was able to find a nature-based thyroid medication and immune system supplements to support my body. Additionally, I had to make intentional changes to my lifestyle and habits, including slowing down, taking regular breaks, and shifting to more mind-body practices like yoga, meditation, breathwork, mindfulness, and Qigong. I also had to change my approach to nutrition by reducing my consumption of inflammatory foods, such as gluten (sigh) and dairy (double sigh).

As van der Kolk shared, the trauma and prolonged stress that we do not work through can change our brain and our nervous system so that we experience our lives in a different way. In this way, trauma is akin to shin splints. I was a long-distance runner in high school and college and experienced shin splints after I stopped running. If you or someone you know has ever experienced shin splints, you will be able to relate to this. If you have never had the pleasure (note: this is sarcasm) of experiencing shin splints, they are caused by repetitive impact on the shin and the surrounding tissues that attach the shinbone to the muscles in the lower leg. Shin splints cause intense pain (understatement of the century) and swelling. For me, my shin splints were caused by running on uneven, hard, and inclined surfaces. Shin splints are wicked painful, but what's even more painful is the residue left behind – the scar tissue. Until that scar tissue is worked out, you continue to have the extreme pain from shin splints even when you are no longer running. Similarly, when trauma and prolonged stress is left unhealed, it can cause changes in your brain and nervous system and your physical body, as van der Kolk and Felitti, among many others, have mentioned.

INTENTIONAL PAUSE

➤ What do I notice in my mind? (observe without judgment)
➤ What do I notice in my body? (observe without judgment)
➤ What do I notice in my feelings? (observe without judgment)
➤ What do I notice in my thoughts? (observe without judgment)
➤ What do I need at this moment to feel supported? (observe without judgment and give yourself what you need to feel supported)

Now that we've explored trauma and the ACEs Study, let's move on to the Polyvagal Theory.

POLYVAGAL THEORY

I found out about Polyvagal Theory in 2010 during my mental health learning adventure. Part of the research that van der Kolk delves into in his book was based on research started by Charles Darwin in the mid- to late-1800s. Based on some of Darwin's work, Dr. Stephen Porges, a well-known expert in developmental psychophysiology and developmental behavioral neuroscience, introduced the Polyvagal Theory in 1994.

Before we take time to understand Polyvagal Theory, I'd like to introduce you to the vagus nerve, a critical focus in the theory. The vagus nerve, which is shown in Figure 2.1, is the 10th cranial nerve and is often referred to as cranial nerve X in medical terms.

Figure 2.1 The brain, in right profile with the glossopharyngeal and vagus nerves, and, to the right, a view of the base of the brain.

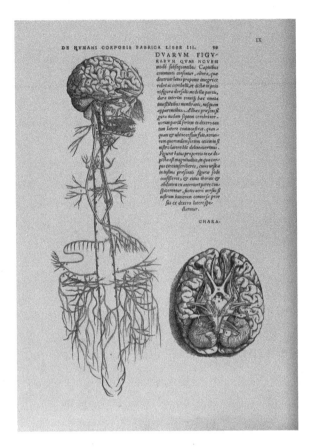

Source: A 1543 woodcut, from the collection of Henry Wellcome. https://wellcome collection.org/works/njv3mjbp.

The word *vagus* means "wandering," and the vagus nerve physically does just that in our bodies – it wanders, and, as it does, it hits every major organ in our body, including our lungs, heart, liver, spleen, stomach, intestines, and kidneys. It really gets around!

What does the vagus nerve do? The vagus nerve is responsible for both sensory and motor functions in the body.

Thus, when our body experiences prolonged stress and trauma, the vagus nerve alerts all the organs it touches about the stressful situation, and, as we've already discussed, when our prolonged stress and trauma are not worked through, physical symptoms and illness arise in our bodies. Therefore, vagus nerve health is essential to whole body health.

Put simply, the Polyvagal Theory centers on our nervous system's activity in our body, including when we feel safe or in danger, and how that affects the way we behave. Polyvagal Theory can also help us explain how we feel, think, and connect with others, which is important to our learning processes. Additionally, it illustrates our reaction to stress. It's important to note that while our bodies are built for stress, they are not built to sustain when we're experiencing chronic, overwhelming stress.

In order to get to higher brain function, we need a solid sensory and emotional foundation. This sensory foundation includes our connection to our five senses as well as our body awareness. This base level also includes our feelings of safety, trust, and connection to ourselves and others. Learning, focus, and communication are truly dependent on our ability to process the information that is entering through our sensory and emotional levels.

There are two additional topics I'd like to cover before we move on from Polyvagal Theory, and those topics include ventral vagal and dorsal vagal.

The ventral (or front) side of the vagus nerve is our sense of safety, while our dorsal (or back) side of our vagus nerve is keyed into danger. The dorsal vagal affects all bodily functioning below the diaphragm, including the digestive system, while the ventral vagal affects everything above the diaphragm. When we're in ventral vagal, we are calm and grounded. When we're in dorsal vagal, we are ready to shut down or run away.

Some of the responses when we're outside of our safe place include fight, flight, freeze, and fawn.

Figure 2.2 Responses when we don't feel safe.

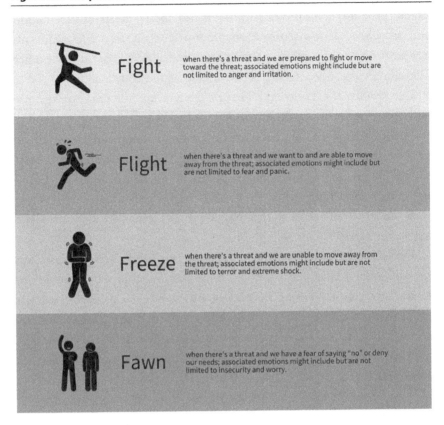

Fight — when there's a threat and we are prepared to fight or move toward the threat; associated emotions might include but are not limited to anger and irritation.

Flight — when there's a threat and we want to and are able to move away from the threat; associated emotions might include but are not limited to fear and panic.

Freeze — when there's a threat and we are unable to move away from the threat; associated emotions might include but are not limited to terror and extreme shock.

Fawn — when there's a threat and we have a fear of saying "no" or deny our needs; associated emotions might include but are not limited to insecurity and worry.

While there is much more to the Polyvagal Theory, this small slice of information is enough to understand the next topic, which is the Window of Tolerance.

WINDOW OF TOLERANCE

The Window of Tolerance, first introduced by Dr. Dan Siegel, is our ability to deal with the ever-changing world around us without losing ourselves in the uncertainty of it all. When we experience prolonged stress and trauma, we can get pushed outside of our Window of Tolerance into hyperarousal or hypoarousal states.

Figure 2.3 Window of Tolerance.

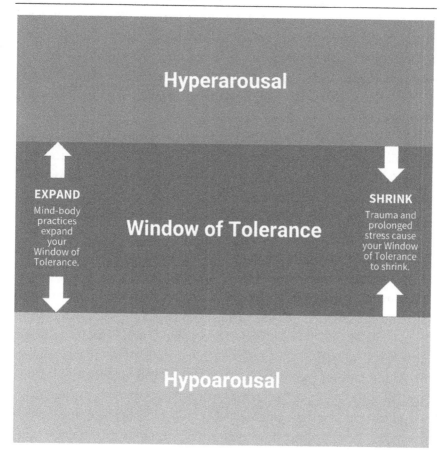

What does it mean to be in a state of hyperarousal? When we're in a state of hyperarousal, among other symptoms, we're likely to experience increased heart rate, rapid breathing, insomnia, racing thoughts, heightened anxiety, feelings of overwhelmingness, increased anger, and an inability to focus. We might feel like we need to run away from something, which is often called our flight response. Sometimes in the hyperarousal state, we are more aggressive and go into a fight response.

What does it mean to be in a state of hypoarousal? When we're in a state of hypoarousal, we can experience a freeze response where we might zone out or do something to distract, disconnect, or withdraw ourselves from whatever is pushing us outside of our ability to cope. We could experience a lack of feelings or energy, difficulty thinking or interacting, decreased movement, feelings of numbness, to name a few. We might go into fawn response, which is also known as please and appease; we ignore our needs, give up on trying to stick up for or support ourselves, and give into others and their influence.

The optimum scenario that we want is to stay within our Window of Tolerance, especially because there is a major implication for education if we don't. Based on Siegel's work, when we're in hyperarousal or hypoarousal (including fight, flight, fawn, and freeze), no new learning can take place. The moral of this story is that growing our Window of Tolerance is critical to our mental health and wellbeing as well as to our learning processes.

When I came to this understanding, I was so relieved because it helped me have compassion for myself for what I experienced during my nervous breakdown. The Window of Tolerance really helped me understand why my mind and body shut down during an overwhelming time and how my past trauma was still residing in the tissues of my body. What it also taught me is that I was safe in the present moment while continuing to support myself and heal my past trauma. As educators, it is vital that we learn to increase our Window of Tolerance, which will, in turn, increase our ability to deal with the constant and inevitable changes in the field of education and in our lives in general, without losing ourselves in the uncertainty of it all.

So what does it take to grow our Window of Tolerance? Exploring more about the brain and how it learns can help us understand what is needed to not only grow our Window of Tolerance, but also heal our trauma and prolonged stress.

THE BRAIN AND LEARNING

The brain includes three layers.

The base layer is focused on safety [Survival (Primal/Reptilian Basal Ganglia)], including internal safety, external safety, and safety in staying in

Figure 2.4 The brain and learning.

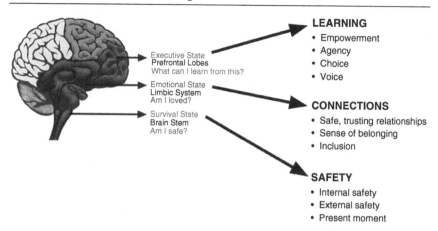

the present moment. Once we have safety, the second layer from the bottom is the opportunity to build trusting relationships and connections, as well as a sense of belonging and inclusion [Emotional (Paleomammalian/ Limbic System)]. After we have our safety and connections, that's when learning can take place [Executive (Neomammalian/Rational/Neocortex)]. Note that there is also a connection between the vagus nerve and the brainstem; the brainstem acts as a gatekeeper, receiving information from the body via the vagus nerve.

As an example of the brain and our learning abilities, let's look at what is happening during the pandemic. To be expected, many schools and districts focused attention on how to continue delivering learning to their students.

What we heard at the same time is that educators and students felt disconnected. The focus was often more on the learning and less on connection, safety, and healing. By putting learning as a priority during the pandemic, there was no time for educators, caregivers, and students to feel safe and to subsequently create trusting relationships and community, which also serve as major contributing factors for both motivation and engagement.

Unfortunately, there continues to be a focus on learning via the field's mantra of "learning loss" and "learning gaps'" rather than on the process of healing during one of the biggest mental health crises experienced in history. As one of our Wellness for Educators' board members, Jonathan Santos Silva, founder and executive director of The Liber Institute, emphasized, there are implications based on the words we use, especially for people of color:

> "Learning loss" and "learning gaps" are deficit-based language that can "other" children, especially those from different backgrounds. The focus on "gaps and losses" reinforces that some learning is valued over others, usually learning associated with mainstream (white) values. For instance, educators and students may have missed content and professional learning that the system deems valuable, but they may have learned valuable lessons from a cultural or familial perspective that they would have otherwise missed if they were stuck in school. This just adds to the unnecessary stress educators and students already carry.

A 2022 Rand report found that pandemic learning loss is the top job-related stressor (Steiner et al.). For the adults, adolescents, and children in the education system, at the neurobiological level, when we feel unsafe, the amygdala becomes activated, which leads the hippocampus to shut down. The hippocampus plays a vital role in learning, memory encoding, and memory consolidation.

The trauma-informed approach is shown on the bottom of Figure 2.5, with the top priority being safety and healing first, then relationship building/connection, and then learning (van der Kolk 2014; Porges 2011). This is really modeled after the idea that "you have to Maslow before you can Bloom." This means that we should be taking care of our basic needs first, including physiological, safety, and connections, so that we have a strong foundation for learning. Unless we have the safety and healing and trusting connections that can support the regulation of our nervous system, learning cannot happen in meaningful and sustained ways (Siegel 1999).

Figure 2.5 Pandemic approach and trauma-informed approach.

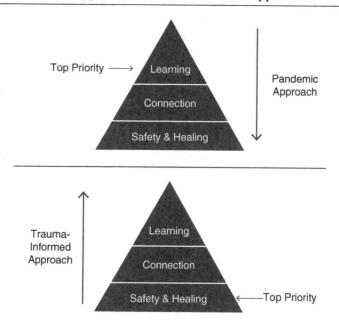

HEALING TRAUMA AND PROLONGED STRESS

Dr. Nadine Burke Harris, author of *The Deepest Well: Healing the Long-Term Effects of Childhood Adversity,* emphasizes that "we have the capacity for neuroplasticity throughout our lives, and our environments shape the way that our brains respond to our experiences. Safe, stable, and nurturing relationships are healing for kids, and for all of us." When practiced regularly, mind-body education and practices can help us cultivate safety, allowing us to create safe connections, and, ultimately, build our Window of Tolerance, and heal trauma and prolonged stress. As Dr. Albert Wong expressed, the field of neuroscience has highlighted mind-body approaches as our inherent self-regulatory processes. Some examples of this include dance, art, singing, movement therapy, body-mind grounding, and play therapy, to name just a few.

These practices enable us to stay in the present moment to understand our sensations, our impulses, and our emotions. Our sensations, impulses, and emotions can really help us build the habits of mind to internally check in with ourselves – supporting us to create that intentional mind-body connection – to understand what is acceptable for us and not. This mind-body connection can also help guide our decisions, relationships, emotions, communications, and more. With the mind-body connection, we can regulate our nervous system, heal, and, in time, change the physiological states that result from trauma and prolonged stress.

For the purposes of this book, we focus on six mind-body connection practices that center on intentional movement – yoga, breathwork, meditation, mindfulness, Qigong, and yin yoga.

Before we get into describing and engaging in these practices, I want to acknowledge the potential elephant in the room, which is critical for ensuring educator wellness. As is mentioned in Chapter 1, educator wellness is not an individual effort; rather, it needs to be a system-level effort, as there are many contributing factors that are outside of educators' control that affect their mental health and wellbeing. Vickie Echols, a retired school administrator and Wellness for Educators' SEL and organizational culture facilitator, shares the continuum of wellness during her mind-body education sessions. The continuum of wellness emphasizes the supports that are needed not only at the individual level, but also at the school and systemic levels.

INTENTIONAL PAUSE

> What do I notice in my mind? (observe without judgment)
> What do I notice in my body? (observe without judgment)
> What do I notice in my feelings? (observe without judgment)
> What do I notice in my thoughts? (observe without judgment)
> What do I need at this moment to feel supported? (observe without judgment and give yourself what you need to feel supported)

In the next chapter, we delve into the school- and systemic-level issues that need to be dealt with in order for true educator wellness to be experienced. Let's dive in!

ADDITIONAL RESOURCES

Trainings

The Embody Lab – http://www.theembodylab.com
National Institute for the Clinical Application of Behavioral Medicine – http://www.nicabm.com
Polyvagal Institute – https://www.polyvagalinstitute.org/
Somatic Abolitionism with Resmaa Menakem – https://www.resmaa.com/
Wellness for Educators – http://well4edu.org

Books

Dr. Nadine Burke Harris – *The Deepest Well: Healing the Long-Term Effects of Childhood Adversity*
Dr. Peter Levine – *Waking the Tiger: Healing Trauma*
Dr. Gabor Maté
- *In the Realm of Hungry Ghosts: Close Encounters with Addiction*
- *Scattered Minds: The Origins and Healing of Attention Deficit Disorder*
Resmaa Menakem – *My Grandmother's Hands: Racialized Trauma and the Pathway to Mending Our Hearts and Bodies*
Dr. Stephen Porges – *The Polyvagal Theory*
Dr. Bessel van der Kolk – *The Body Keeps the Score: Brain, Mind, and Body in the Healing of Trauma*

CHAPTER 3

Elephant in the (Class)room: School- and Systemic-Level Issues

Disclaimer: By writing this book, I am not saying that all you have to do to preserve your mental health and well-being as an educator is engage in yoga, breathwork, meditation, Qigong, yin yoga, and mindfulness. That would be an epic form of gaslighting[1] and spiritual bypassing.[2]

What I am saying is to preserve your mental health and wellbeing, you must be aware not only of your own need for healing, but also of how systemic- and school-level issues that you may, or, more likely than not, may not have any control over can be managed. In the case where you do have some control over affecting change, you have options.

In the case where you do not have control over something, you may also have the option to work with someone who could effect change. If there's no ability to effect meaningful change, and the issue affects your mental health and wellbeing, it may be necessary to leave the space and shift to a place that is more supportive. As Dr. Thema Bryant-Davis, president of the American Psychological Association, expressed, "Start prioritizing your mental health instead of adjusting to toxic spaces."

Figure 3.1 Toxic spaces.

Source: Monkey Business / Adobe Stock

This chapter shares a brief overview of school- and systemic-level issues that have been studied for decades, if not longer. This chapter does not serve as an exhaustive list of all the issues, but it acknowledges what has been reported in the research.

The vital importance of educator wellness was by no means a new topic when Wellness for Educators started in 2019. Studies in the early 1980s explored the need for school health programs focused on combating rising educator attrition rates (Allensworth and Kolbe 1987). Research from the 1990s and 2000s reported educators experiencing pressure from multiple sources, including but not limited to:

- high-stakes testing (Ball 2003; Hargreaves 2003)
- excessive workload (Cazes, Hijzen, and Saint-Martin 2015; Kinnunen and Salo 1994; Bakker et al. 2007; Hakanen, Bakker, and Schaufeli 2006; OECD 2013)
- large class sizes (UIS 2016)
- inadequate resources (Mostafa and Pál 2018)
- student behavioral challenges (McCallum et al. 2017; McCallum and Price 2010)
- poor physical space (Buckley 2004; Earthman and Lemasters 2009; Hakanen, Bakker, and Schaufeli 2006)
- lack of support (McCallum et al. 2017)

This is, unfortunately, not an exhaustive list.

Prolonged stress and trauma caused by the issues shared here and more have led to educator attrition (Borman and Dowling 2008; Craig 2017; McCallum et al. 2017; Carver-Thomas and Darling-Hammond 2017; McCallum and Price 2010).

Figure 3.2 Trauma and prolonged stress effect on educator attrition.

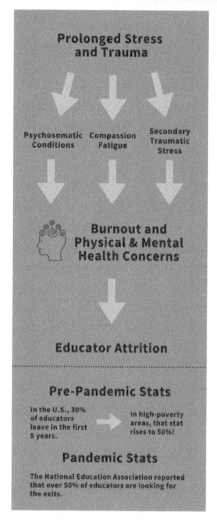

Sources: Borman and Dowling 2008; Craig 2017; McCallum et al. 2017; Carver-Thomas and Darling-Hammond 2017; McCallum and Price 2010; Cochran-Smith 2004; Ingersoll 2003; McCallum et al. 2017; Jotkoff 2022.

Educators of color and culture and those who identify as LGBTQIA+ are at even greater risk of leaving the field (Carver-Thomas and Darling-Hammond 2017; U.S. Department of Education 2016), and given the supporting research on the impact representation has in promoting safety and connection, the exodus of these educators, in particular, is most worrisome for our students of color and culture and those who identify as LGBTQIA+.

In recent years and especially during the pandemic, the field reported educator shortages. While research has shown that there have been educator shortages off and on throughout history, more recently, educators have noted that even more alarming than the educator shortage is the field's inability to retain educators.

The issues affecting educator wellbeing are organized using the Teacher Wellbeing Model, which was outlined in an Organisation for Economic Co-operation and Development (OECD) white paper in 2020 (Viac and Fraser 2020). There are also policy categories within the OECD paper. While the paper is focused on educator wellness, it acknowledges how educator wellness is affected by many other contributing factors in the educators' leading, teaching, supporting, and learning environments and beyond.

Figure 3.3 Educator Wellbeing Model.

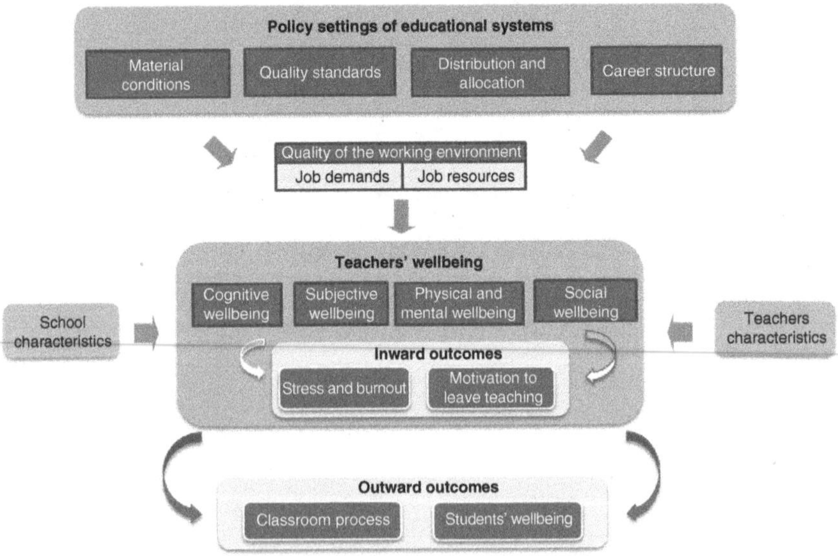

Source: Viac and Fraser 2020.

For the purposes of this book, I expanded this model to focus on educators in general rather than teachers specifically. All educators, including leaders, teachers, and other supporting educators, suffer from burnout, trauma, and prolonged stress, especially in the midst of the pandemic, not only because they are diminishing their own reserves to serve others, but also because of these underlying school-level and systemic issues.

Viac and Fraser share four categories of educator wellbeing, including the following: Cognitive Wellbeing, Subjective Wellbeing, Physical and Mental Wellbeing, and Social Wellbeing.

Figure 3.4 Four categories of educator wellbeing.

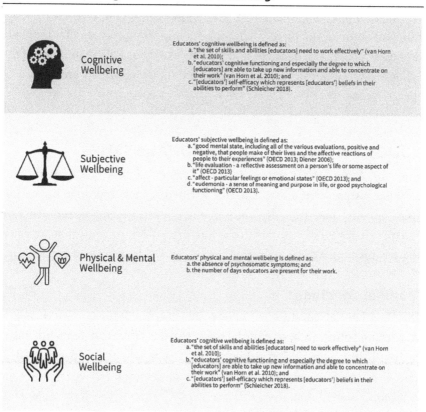

Cognitive Wellbeing

Educators' cognitive wellbeing is defined as:
a. "the set of skills and abilities [educators] need to work effectively" (van Horn et al. 2010);
b. "educators' cognitive functioning and especially the degree to which [educators] are able to take up new information and able to concentrate on their work" (van Horn et al. 2010); and
c. "[educators'] self-efficacy which represents [educators'] beliefs in their abilities to perform" (Schleicher 2018).

Subjective Wellbeing

Educators' subjective wellbeing is defined as:
a. "good mental state, including all of the various evaluations, positive and negative, that people make of their lives and the affective reactions of people to their experiences" (OECD 2013; Diener 2006);
b. "life evaluation - a reflective assessment on a person's life or some aspect of it" (OECD 2013)
c. "affect - particular feelings or emotional states" (OECD 2013); and
d. "eudemonia - a sense of meaning and purpose in life, or good psychological functioning" (OECD 2013).

Physical & Mental Wellbeing

Educators' physical and mental wellbeing is defined as:
a. the absence of psychosomatic symptoms; and
b. the number of days educators are present for their work.

Social Wellbeing

Educators' cognitive wellbeing is defined as:
a. "the set of skills and abilities [educators] need to work effectively" (van Horn et al. 2010);
b. "educators' cognitive functioning and especially the degree to which [educators] are able to take up new information and able to concentrate on their work" (van Horn et al. 2010); and
c. "[educators'] self-efficacy which represents [educators'] beliefs in their abilities to perform" (Schleicher 2018).

Source: Viac and Fraser 2020.

Many contributing factors feed into the four categories of educator wellbeing and are organized into two areas that are discussed in detail in the next section:

- Policy settings of educational systems
- Quality of the working environment (Viac and Fraser 2020)

In addition to these school-level issues, there are systemic-level issues at national and global levels. These factors can contribute individually to educators' wellbeing and to educators' decision to stay in the field or leave. Because they affect educator wellbeing, these factors can also have the potential to contribute to students' wellbeing.

The remainder of this chapter gives a brief overview of these contributing factors that cause educators to leave the profession. Again, this chapter does not provide an exhaustive list of reasons for educator attrition, but provides some of the most cited ones. It's important to note that there are organizations, states, districts, and schools working to alleviate some of the school- and system-level issues, some examples of which are shared in this chapter.

POLICY SETTINGS OF EDUCATIONAL SYSTEMS

Viac and Fraser share four areas that categorize policy settings of educational systems that affect educator wellbeing, including material conditions, quality standards, distribution and allocation, and career structure (2020). Their research points to the fractures in our systems that are causing serious issues.

Material Conditions

ISSUE: Material conditions include, but are not limited to, low salary. According to research, one of the main reasons educators report dissatisfaction in their profession is low salary (Collie, Shapka, and Perry 2012; OECD 2014). For instance, a study conducted by the National Center for Education Statistics showed that teachers who made less than $40,000 to start were 10% more likely to leave the profession than those who earned over that (Gray and Taie 2015). Educators of color make markedly less than white educators (Carver-Thomas and Darling-Hammond, 2017; U.S. Department of Education, 2016).

OPTIONS: A competitive salary can make a difference. Viac and Fraser point to literature on what a competitive salary can do to improve attraction of highly experienced teacher candidates (Hendricks 2015), increase in work productivity (Britton and Propper 2016), and student success (Akiba et al. 2012; Hendricks 2014). Policy makers need this research in hand as they make decisions about how to allocate funds for schools and districts that align with district goals.

Quality Standards

ISSUE: Multiple sets of standards and policies exist for educators from national, state, and local levels. Standards exist not only for specific educator professionals, but also for content-specific and context-specific purposes. These standards oftentimes are used for evaluation purposes. While standards are vital to uphold quality and accountability in a system, they can also cause educator stress. Additionally, the number of standards to follow can also lead to educators not having time and space for agency and creativity.

OPTIONS: Standards can be used when necessary to set clear goals to be measured, to inform instruction, and to align to student achievement. However, when they are getting in the way of educator and student wellbeing, how they are used should be revisited in order to promote a safe space for leading, teaching, and learning. Additionally, when we think about how everyday work requires collaboration and connection, should this prompt us to look differently at the way we assess students so that it is more in line with what is happening outside of standardized tests?

Distribution and Allocation

ISSUE: Educators have so much on their plates, which often leads to work overload (Cazes, Hijzen, and Saint-Martin 2015; Kinnunen and Salo 1994; Bakker et al. 2007; Hakanen et al. 2006; OECD 2013) and lack of adequate resources (Mostafa and Pál 2018). There is always a new initiative that schools and districts want to incorporate in order to continue to improve.

OPTIONS: While innovation is exciting and essential, systems can think critically about what they can take off educators' plates as they add on new things. In the instance of large class sizes, for example, which is another one of the primary reasons educators leave the profession (UIS 2016), some districts and schools are using unique approaches like blended learning, project-based learning, and team teaching to alleviate educator overload. Schools and districts might also consider role consolidation. Many educators have asked their schools to consider taking tasks off their plates. Because of the many requirements that schools have to meet at the district and state levels, we know that this is often not possible. What is possible for schools, however, is the opportunity to consolidate educator roles. Doing this not only helps alleviate the pressure that educators feel when trying to juggle many roles, but it also provides teachers an opportunity to step into teacher leadership. This option of role consolidation also illustrates the power of educator autonomy, opening up space for educators to innovate and be creative. When educators feel empowered and supported, their job satisfaction rises, and subsequently, they are more likely to stay (OECD 2014; OECD 2019). Role consolidation is not only a way to retain educators but also an opportunity to bolster educators and strengthen school culture.

Career Structure

ISSUE: One reason most cited for educator attrition is lack of upward mobility (McCallum et al. 2017). In some cases, schools and districts do not have many opportunities for promotion.

OPTIONS: Because of this, some states have established a program that provides leadership roles for professionals within and outside of their immediate campus or district. For instance, the role of teacher leader has provided many systems with ways to empower educators who want to advance and lead when there are no specific ways to do so in their own school or district. Some teachers are also moving to positions such as SEL specialists or instructional coaches.

QUALITY OF THE WORKING ENVIRONMENT

Multiple Roles

ISSUE: An additional contributing factor that is cited as leading to educator attrition at the school level includes educators playing multiple roles or wearing too many hats (Viac and Fraser 2020).

OPTIONS: Some schools and districts are working on this by looking at the roles that each educator plays and how the responsibilities are distributed; they ask educators to choose the responsibilities that most align with their interests so they can become a leader in that area.

Another way schools and districts are supporting educators to not take on too much is by hiring someone to coordinate a program and support educators with implementation. For instance, if you bring in a social emotional learning (SEL) and mental health program to a district, instead of asking every educator to become experts in SEL and mental health, the school might hire an SEL and mental health coordinator who then supports the educators with lesson ideas like the role an educational technology specialist plays alongside educators as they integrate technology in meaningful ways. Role consolidation can also work here, as was mentioned in the "Distribution and Allocation" section.

Physical Environment and Student Behavior

ISSUE: Other job demands that lead to educator attrition include but are not limited to physical learning environments (noise, lighting, dirt, air quality, temperature, to name a few) as well as student behavioral challenges (McCallum et al. 2017; McCallum and Price 2010). With the amount of prolonged stress and trauma all stakeholders have felt during the pandemic, it's not surprising that student behavioral challenges have been on the rise.

OPTIONS: A key in supporting students as they experience challenging emotions and experiences is to have restorative practices and spaces at the ready. Examples include designing a calming/Zen room or BeWell Room (see one of Wellness for Educators' Partner nonprofits BeWell in School, based in Nashville, Tennessee). These types of de-stressing spaces are helpful for educators as well.

Pressure from Evaluation

ISSUE: Performance evaluation has come up in research as another reason educators have chosen to leave the field. For some educators, their evaluation's direct alignment with their students' success on high-stakes testing is too much pressure not only on them but also on students (Ball 2003; Hargreaves 2003). In some cases, evaluations are also tied to compensation, adding another layer of stress.

OPTIONS: On the flip side of the demands are the resources that schools and districts can provide. One option shared by Viac and Fraser is work autonomy. Autonomy allows the educator space to innovate and be creative. Another way is to offer support for training and other professional opportunities, such as attending professional conferences. Some schools and districts have implemented mentoring programs; research has shown that support systems like mentoring programs can lead to job satisfaction and provide social support, feedback, and appraisal (Bakker et. al 2007; OECD 2014).

SYSTEMIC ISSUES

In addition to the school-level issues previously mentioned, there are systemic issues in the community that can and do impact educator wellness. The three most noted in the field of education currently include gun violence, racism, and gender discrimination.

Gun Violence

According to the Center for Homeland Defense and Security Naval Postgraduate School's K–12 School Shooting Database, from 1970 through June 2022, the United States has reported 2,068 school shootings, with 1,934 injuries and 684 deaths.[3] The latest one as I write this chapter happened at Robb Elementary School in Uvalde, Texas, where 22 people died, including 19 children. One teacher, who was also shot but survived, was in the room while 11 of his students were shot to death. Putting aside all the politics involved in gun control and just reflecting on the terror, fear, grief, and anger, what does it feel like to be a teacher right now?

The following is a poem that a friend of mine, Emily Baker, wrote. She's an early childhood teacher in Maine. This is her reflection after the school shooting on May 24, 2022, in Uvalde, Texas:

I AM A TEACHER

I protect little voices and big feelings.
I am not bulletproof.
I am a Teacher.
I wear snot on my shoulder right next to my heart.
I clean away exhausted tears.
I am not bulletproof.
I am a Teacher.
I give tools to little hands so that they can carry the weight of
    our future.
I am not bulletproof.
I am a Teacher.
I light a match to curiosity and provide blueprints to connection.
I am not bulletproof.
I am a Teacher.
I am a Home for some.
I am a full belly.
I am safety and comfort.
I am glitter bombs and celebration.
I am a Teacher.
You can give me a gun
and make me replace sanctuary with fear, but
I will never be bulletproof.

– Emily Baker

She and many other educators around the world went back to school the day after this event and the many others before it. How could they tell their students they are safe when they themselves can't be sure of that? Even when educators are not in the same building in which a shooting has taken place, they feel the trauma and experience vicarious trauma (secondary traumatic stress), compassion fatigue, and prolonged stress as if they were. Safety is not having to worry about being shot at work.

Many schools and districts have implemented active shooter drills, which in and of themselves can also be extremely traumatizing. Compounding is the experience of vicarious trauma or secondary traumatic stress when educators hear their students share their reflections and experiences.

Revisiting the importance of safety in the learning process from Chapter 2: for the adults, adolescents, and children in the education system, at the neurobiological level, when we feel unsafe, the amygdala becomes activated, which leads the hippocampus to shut down. The hippocampus plays a vital role in learning, memory encoding, and memory consolidation. When we feel unsafe, our learning processes are affected. *Safety is needed for learning to take place.*

INTENTIONAL PAUSE

- ➤ What do I notice in my mind? (observe without judgment)
- ➤ What do I notice in my body? (observe without judgment)
- ➤ What do I notice in my feelings? (observe without judgment)
- ➤ What do I notice in my thoughts? (observe without judgment)
- ➤ What do I need at this moment to feel supported? (observe without judgment and give yourself what you need to feel supported)

Racism

Racism is another major systemic issue that is making learning spaces unsafe for educators and their students. One of my somatic experiencing teachers, Dr. Sherri Mitchell Weh'na Ha'mu Kwasset, who is of the Penobscot Nation and serves as an Indigenous rights' activist and lawyer, shared that the first step in her many years of therapy was to establish a baseline of accepting her right to exist. As Nelson Mandela said during an address to the Joint Houses of Parliament at Westminster Hall in London in July 1996, "Racism is a blight on the human conscience. The idea that any people can be inferior to another, to the point where those who consider themselves superior define and treat the rest as subhuman, denies the humanity even of those who elevate themselves to the status of gods." A lifetime of racism and carrying ancestral trauma brought on by racism, as Mandela said, has made people of color feel "subhuman." As Dr. Méroudjie Denis, Wellness for Educators' chair of the Board of Directors says, "Many people of color struggle with existing in a world that sees us as 'subhuman' and, even when we value our existence, we wrestle with the notion that others do not recognize, nor value our full humanity." Dr. Denis said:

> With every senseless massacre of Black people in America, I am reminded that being Black in America feels like you are walking around with a gaping wound that never gets a chance to heal. By the time you stop the bleeding and clean the wound, someone comes along to punch you in the same place, reopening that wound and having you start the process all over again. The worst part is after they have punched you, they try to convince you there was never a wound to begin with and you are left watching yourself bleed out, knowing another punch is coming. All the while wondering, when will my life matter to you? (Personal correspondence July 31, 2022)

Racism is rampant in the current political climate. Some states are creating laws forbidding educators to discuss culture and race in their learning environments. Books and curriculum are being banned that outline the true history of white oppression, structural racism, and slavery. Additionally, as Jonathan Santos Silva, founder and executive director of The Liber Institute and a member of Wellness for Educators Board of Directors, said, "The missed opportunity is not just to tell the truth about oppressors but also the freedom fighters and civil rights activists of all backgrounds, including white abolitionists, freedom riders, and allies across our history." There have been cases where school board members and educators have been threatened by communities when they oppose racism outright. In some cases, this leads to conflict in the school or district when there's a conflict between parental rights versus educators' professionalism. There are concerted efforts of some communities to remove their school from a unified progressive district in order to have more control over what their children learn.

When you know that safety is needed for learning to take place, you also start to think differently about achievement gaps. Trauma causes our ability to learn to go offline. Experiencing continuous macro- and microaggressions, racialized trauma can be, and, unfortunately, typically is a daily experience for people of color, making them feel unsafe and potentially affecting their ability to learn.

Revisiting the importance of safety in the learning process from Chapter 2: for the adults, adolescents, and children in the education system, at the neurobiological level, when we feel unsafe, the amygdala becomes activated, which leads the hippocampus to shut down. The hippocampus plays a vital role in learning, memory encoding, and memory consolidation. When we feel unsafe, our learning processes are affected. *Safety is needed for learning to take place.*

Gender Discrimination

Like racism, the experience of gender discrimination for those in the LGBTQIA+ community is nothing short of dehumanizing. In 2022, 13 states – Florida, Alabama, Ohio, Louisiana, Georgia, Tennessee, Kentucky,

Indiana, Oklahoma, Missouri, South Carolina, Iowa, and Texas – proposed "Don't Say Gay" bills. Some bills also prohibit educating K–12 students about gender identity and diversity. As part of an NPR member station interview, Kathryn Poe of Equality Ohio commented on the Ohio bill when it was proposed:

> When we segment children off and tell them that they don't exist and that they don't matter and effectively erase them from the classroom and say that they can't share their experiences and their home lives in school – we effectively erase them. We alienate an entire group of young people who need our affirmation and support.

Poe's sentiments also transfer to those educators who represent the LGBTQIA+ community as well as those who are allies and want to support their LGBTQIA+ students. In 2021, The Trevor Project found that 42% of people ages 13–24 in the LGBTQIA+ community seriously attempted to commit suicide in 2020. One of the biggest issues I see is if educators from the LGBTQIA+ community leave, that will take away even more sense of safety from students in that community. As we know from research, representation matters.

Revisiting the importance of safety in the learning process from Chapter 2: for the adults, adolescents, and children in the education system, at the neurobiological level, when we feel unsafe, the amygdala becomes activated, which leads the hippocampus to shut down. The hippocampus plays a vital role in learning, memory encoding, and memory consolidation. When we feel unsafe, our learning processes are affected. *Safety is needed for learning to take place.*

There are many more systemic issues that affect educators and the communities they serve. This chapter only shares a tip of the iceberg. The issues shared shed even more light on the need for educator wellness to be more than an individual effort. Educator wellness needs to be a system-level effort.

Research shows that system changes and school-wide wellness programs that include support for every stakeholder have led to positive impacts on educators and the system at large, including but not limited to:

- improvement of educator mental and physical health (Ross and Wu 1995)
- decreases in anxiety, stress, and absenteeism (Collie et al. 2015; Klassen et al. 2009)
- improved school culture (CDC 2012; GENYOUth 2013; Kolbe 2002)
- educator job satisfaction (Moore Johnson 2012)
- increased student outcomes (Harris et al. 2016)

It's important to note that school-wide wellness programs can sometimes be implemented in a way to control and oppress educators and students. For instance, social emotional learning is sometimes used to quiet students' voices or make them think that feelings are not important to express. That makes it vitally important to be intentional by leading with equity in the implementation process and being mindful of centering belonging, inclusion, trust, and safety. Approaching school-wide wellness programs in this way ensures that healing and liberation are the goals rather than trauma, shame, isolation, and stress.

In some places, conservative politics have turned "social emotional learning," "trauma," and "mental health" into bad words. Educators engaged in a system-wide wellness program can make their own shifts by focusing on respect, collaboration, connection, and relationship-building.

A video from The Trauma Foundation conveyed the impact of trauma on our collective population:

> Collectively, we have an epidemic of social issues that are rooted in trauma. If we can do the work to heal past traumas and build healthy, regulated nervous systems as individuals, families, and communities, we can end the cycles that continue to reinforce our greatest challenges and create a safer, vibrant, and more connected world. (Trauma and the Nervous System, 8:22)

The full video is available on YouTube at https://youtu.be/ZdIQRxwT1I0.

A major part of a wellness program puzzle needs to be mind-body practices. Before we dive into learning more about their origin and how to practice them, we explore the research behind them.

INTENTIONAL PAUSE

- ➤ What do I notice in my mind? (observe without judgment)
- ➤ What do I notice in my body? (observe without judgment)
- ➤ What do I notice in my feelings? (observe without judgment)
- ➤ What do I notice in my thoughts? (observe without judgment)
- ➤ What do I need at this moment to feel supported? (observe without judgment and give yourself what you need to feel supported)

NOTES

1. *Gaslighting*: "psychological manipulation of a person usually over an extended period of time that causes the victim to question the validity of their own thoughts, perception of reality, or memories and typically leads to confusion, loss of confidence and self-esteem, uncertainty of one's emotional or mental stability, and a dependency on the perpetrator." In many gaslighting situations, there is a power dynamic involved between the perpetrator and the victim. In the case of educator wellness, this can take the form of the education system's use of toxic positivity.

2. *Spiritual bypassing*: "spiritual ideas and practices to sidestep personal, emotional 'unfinished business,' to shore up a shaky sense of self, or to belittle basic needs, feelings, and developmental tasks" (Welwood 2002). This phenomenon can also be used to bypass systemic issues.
3. https://www.chds.us/ssdb/data-map/.

CHAPTER 4

Mind-Body Practices: What the Research Says

In the last couple of decades, research on the benefits associated with mind-body practices has grown. When we talk about mind-body practices in our work at Wellness for Educators, we are referring to practices that intentionally connect the mind and the body for mental health and overall wellbeing. According to the National Center for Complementary and Integrative Health, mind-body practices "focus on the interactions among the brain, mind, body, and behavior with the intent to use the mind to affect physical functioning and promote health." In this chapter, I share some of the research that has been done on each of the mind-body practices discussed in this book, including yoga, breathwork, meditation, mindfulness, Qigong, and yin yoga. As with the previous research-based chapters, this is not a literature review. This is just a small selection of results from the growing body of research that has been conducted on mind-body practices, and how they can support educator mental health and wellbeing. It's important to note that some of the research results shared in this chapter are focused on students. While this might not look like a direct alignment with educator wellbeing, as shared in Chapter 3, educator wellbeing is a system-level issue, not an individual one. So there are a collection of contributing factors, including student and school wellness. Additionally, we know from research that a person who is in a state of hyper- or hypoarousal can negatively affect a person with a regulated nervous system; thus, any proven effort to support the nervous system is important to share not only for that individual, but also for others around them and the overall environment at large.

RESEARCH ON YOGA

Research on yoga in schools has shown it has positive effects on student test scores, grade point averages (Hagins and Rundle 2016), and disciplinary reports, as well as community and connection in schools as a whole. Yoga also has the potential to support emotion regulation, sense of control, and self-efficacy during stressful times, which can lead to increased resilience (Butzer and Flynn 2018).

Many people first gravitate toward yoga for the physical benefits. Because yoga involves low-impact, weight-bearing activities where muscle and bone experience tension, yoga works to strengthen bones and improve bone density when practiced over time. By improving bone density, people who practice yoga can experience lower risk of fractures and an increase in muscle strength and balance.

Yoga postures typically work multiple muscle groups at one time, which provides an opportunity for the muscles surrounding the joints to strengthen and stretch. This ultimately protects joints, lessens the risk of injury, and, in some cases, has the potential to delay or prevent arthritis. Additionally, as joints and the cartilage within the joint grow accustomed to the added support from bones and muscles, flexibility, function, and range of motion may improve as well.

Yoga has also been found to reduce musculoskeletal pain (Monson et al. 2017). In one study, participants attended bi-weekly, 60-minute yoga sessions for 13 weeks. Across participants, there was a significant decrease in musculoskeletal pain ($p<0.0001$). Research has shown how yoga can also support lower-back and neck pain in addition to supporting the relief of tension-type headaches (Anheyer et al. 2020; Li et al. 2019; Qaseem et al. 2017).

Practicing yoga can also help reduce stress, and, because of this effect, studies have shown that yoga can help lower blood pressure and lessen other stress-related health risks. In a 2016 study, for instance, researchers shared the results of the Lifestyle Modification and Blood Pressure Study (LIMBS) (Cohen et al. 2016). After 12 weeks of bi-weekly 90-minute yoga classes, 180 minutes of walking each week, and a health education program, including nutrition-based guidance, the group saw drops in blood pressure from all participants.

While many people come to yoga for physical exercise, the mind benefits are vast. As previously mentioned, yoga can help reduce stress. Many studies have also noted yoga's ability to reduce anxiety and depression (Zheng and Keltner 2020). Using MRI to examine gray matter in the brain, studies have shown how yoga shifts brain chemistry, reducing gray matter and making room for positive states of joy and happiness (Villemure et al. 2015). Yoga's effects on heart rate variability and vagus nerve stimulation show a tendency toward compassion and kindness, as well as overall health, bringing us from existing in our sympathetic nervous system, where we are on high alert, into our parasympathetic nervous system, where we can come into a calmer state of being.

RESEARCH ON BREATHWORK

Technically, breathwork is part of yoga, as Chapter 5 discusses. In yoga, breathwork is known as *pranayama*. Because the breath can have such a significant effect on our wellbeing, I separate it as its own practice for the book. There are other forms of breathwork outside of the yoga discipline, however, which is another reason why I dedicated a full chapter to it.

Many classrooms have incorporated breathwork into daily routines and have shown positive results. Survey results about the impact of breathwork introduced in accounting and biology classes indicated that students felt that the practice of deep breathing at the start of each class helped them reduce stress, develop a sense of connectedness, and improve focus (Rajkumar, Dubowy, and Khatib 2021).

Breathwork is one practice that helps stimulate the vagus nerve, a strategy that has been shown to reduce stress (Gerritsen and Band 2018). In a study with 29 participants, a four-month training program using yoga-based respiratory exercises showed to improve heart rate variability, which led to improved cardiovascular and respiratory function, including absorption of oxygen (Zheng and Keltner 2020). Different types of breathing can have varying effects on our thinking, feeling, and behavior (Bullock 2019), as is discussed in Chapter 6, "Breathwork."

When we're in the throes of anxiety, oftentimes we go to the same behaviors that brought us there in the first place – overthinking and distraction. When we shift to focus on breathing, we are "bypassing the complexities of the mind and targeting the body directly" (Newman 2020). A study conducted in 2017 brought together a group of people experiencing high levels of anxiety. After taking a course focused on diaphragmatic breathing relaxation, which they practiced twice a day for eight weeks, they reported feeling less anxious. Their physical signs also included a lower heart rate and slower breathing overall (Newman 2020). Specific breathing practices, such as box breathing, have been known to help people fall asleep and relieve insomnia.

RESEARCH ON MEDITATION

Another facet of yoga that I've separated for the purposes of the practices shared in this book is meditation. Meditation in yoga is known as *dhyana*. Similar to breathwork, there are other forms of meditation outside of the yoga discipline, which is why I dedicated a full chapter to it.

Findings from research indicate that meditation is effective in reducing educator burnout, psychological distress, and fatigue factors, and in increasing associated resilience (Valosek et al. 2021).

Since you can choose to engage in a form of meditation while practicing yoga and breathwork, the benefits of those two practices apply in this meditation section, including the reduction of stress, anxiety, and depression. Research also shows that meditation can enhance your memory and attention skills. The practice of meditation can also increase our compassion toward ourselves and others (Simon-Thomas 2013). Meditation can be a dedicated space to practice self-compassion and steer us away from negative self-talk. Meditation has been found to reduce inflammatory response that is caused by stress, which, in turn, reduces blood pressure, fatigue, and brain fog (Rosenkranz et al. 2013).

Meditation can help us stay in the present moment. As Gabor Maté shares in his book *In the Realm of Hungry Ghosts: Close Encounters with Addiction*, "Choice begins the moment you disidentify from the mind and its conditioned patterns, the moment you become present. . . . In present awareness we are liberated from the past." Oftentimes, as mentioned previously, meditation and breath are combined into the same practice to keep us in the present moment. Bessel van der Kolk shares how our meditation on our breath, the awareness we bring to it, can in and of itself be progress: "Many of our patients are barely aware of their breath, so learning to focus on the in and out breath, to notice whether the breath was fast or slow, and to count breaths in some poses can be a significant accomplishment" (2014, p. 272).

RESEARCH ON MINDFULNESS

Similar to the benefits that have been shared for the other practices we've covered so far, mindfulness has been shown to lower blood pressure. Using a course in mindfulness meditation, one study showed significant reduction in systolic and diastolic blood pressure (Suttie 2018). Mindfulness programs have also been shown to reduce stress, pain, anxiety, and depression (Suttie 2018; Halliwell 2018).

Mindfulness has also been shown to support those who are in addiction treatment, providing a structure for understanding cravings. Our social wellbeing is also affected positively by mindfulness practice, causing us to improve our relationships with others (Suttie 2018). Practicing mindfulness also can heighten our awareness and focus our attention.

RESEARCH ON QIGONG

Because it is one of the lesser-known practices shared in this book, I'd like to provide a short description of what Qigong is, even though there is more information shared in Chapter 9. Qigong and yoga tend to be placed in the same category of contemplative practices in modern day medicine, and, specifically, in the integrative health space. Qigong and yoga practices have similar benefits. The practice of Qigong stems from Traditional Chinese Medicine (TCM). TCM "is a range of medicine practices sharing common concepts which have been originated and developed in China, including various forms of acupuncture, dietary therapy, herbal medicine, moxibustion, and physical exercise, which collectively predate to the birth of Chinese civilization" (Wang 2016).

Research shows that Qigong helps practitioners "center in their bodies," bringing people out of their analytical and cognitive processes (Halpern 2010). Because of its static and dynamic forms, Qigong has similar benefits to meditation and movement (Tsang et al. 2002; Shinnick 2006). Qigong, much like the other practices introduced thus far, is known to reduce stress and increase focus (Wayne and Fuerst 2013).

Like yoga, Qigong can increase both lower- and upper-body muscle strength, and, depending on the kind of Qigong being practiced, when done regularly, it has been known to have the same effects as resistance training and brisk walking on practitioners' physical health (Li et al. 2014). In addition to strength, Qigong can also increase flexibility and balance (Jahnke et al. 2010). Qigong practices have also been shown to lower heart rate and improve other cardiovascular and respiratory functions, including breathing frequency (Guichen, Hua, and Zhang 2014; Sun 1988).

The reduction of stress, like the other mind-body practices, also has the potential to reduce inflammation, especially for those who are living with autoimmune disorders as well as other chronic pain conditions, such as fibromyalgia, osteoarthritis, and rheumatoid arthritis (Guichen, Hua, and Zhang 2014). Improved brain function, sleep quality, and immune system functionality have also been noted in a variety of studies (Nordqvist 2021).

Many who practice Qigong have found it an effective treatment in reducing depression (Tsang et al. 2003; Wang, C.W., et al. 2013; Wang, F., et al. 2013; Yeung et al. 2013; Yin and Dishman 2014; Liu et al. 2015; Martinez et al. 2015), anxiety disorders (Lee et al. 2004a, 2004b; Abbott and Lavretsky 2013; Chan et al. 2013), post-traumatic disorders (Grodin et al. 2008; Kim et al. 2013), and burnout (Stenlund et al. (2009; 2012).

RESEARCH ON YIN YOGA

Yin yoga is a discipline that stems from two spaces – Taoist and yogic philosophy. Yin yoga is done mainly on the floor and involves holding of postures in order to lubricate the tissues, allowing the joints and fascia (connective tissues) to move more freely. The static holding of the postures for extended amounts of time creates synovial fluid. The physical benefits of the practice include improved range of motion and flexibility, strengthening of ligaments, reduction of stress and anxiety, boosting of circulation, promotion of relaxation, improvement of sleep, balancing of the internal organs and supporting the flow of chi (energy), and providing space to balance emotions (Clark 2012).

There is much more research on the effects of these mind-body practices. I hope this chapter gives you a jumping off point if you'd like to learn more.

INTENTIONAL PAUSE

> ➤ What do I notice in my mind? (observe without judgment)
> ➤ What do I notice in my body? (observe without judgment)
> ➤ What do I notice in my feelings? (observe without judgment)
> ➤ What do I notice in my thoughts? (observe without judgment)
> ➤ What do I need at this moment to feel supported? (observe without judgment and give yourself what you need to feel supported)

PREPARATION FOR THE PRACTICES

In the next five chapters, we'll explore each of the five disciplines, identify each one's key concepts, and engage in several practices. As you do these practices, it's vital to approach them intentionally. What do I mean by that? I like to use three approaches.

The first approach is to ask just two simple questions.

- What do I notice (in my body and/or mind)? (observe without judgment)
- What do I need in this moment? (observe without judgment and give yourself what you need to feel supported)

The second approach I use when a practice gets tough for me is to refer to Deb Dana's four Rs from her book, *The Polyvagal Theory in Therapy: Engaging the Rhythm of Regulation*:

1. **Recognize the autonomic state.** (How is my nervous system doing? Am I in flight/fight/freeze/fawn?)

2. **Respect the adaptive survival response.** (How am I reacting? Am I crying, shaking, feeling anxious? Whatever it is, the response is what it needs to be. I am not judging it.)

3. **Regulate or co-regulate into a ventral vagal state.** (What does my body and mind need now to feel safe? Do I need to hug myself? Do I need to lie down with my head on a pillow? Do I need a blanket to cover myself?)

4. **Re-story** (How can I re-frame my experience to see the learning that came up for me? What am I telling myself?)

What does this look like in the practice? Take, for example, one of the postures in yin yoga that I don't enjoy very much: Toe Squat.

Toe squat is the bane of my existence. I resist it like no other posture. When I am in it, I go into flight and fight. The posture makes me want to jump out of the present moment. Instead of doing just that, I take notice of how I'm feeling and respect my response. Then, I use my deep breathing to regulate myself. I also allow myself to pull back the intensity, as you should when practicing yin yoga, and practice self-compassion. Then, I re-story by thinking differently, opening my mind a bit more to the possibilities that the posture (and the present moment) is trying to teach me. Oftentimes it's a piece of my story, as Peter Levine shares in *Healing Trauma: A Pioneering Program for Restoring the Wisdom of Your Body*, "The symptoms of trauma can be stable, that is, ever-present. They can also be unstable, meaning that they can come and go and be triggered by stress. Or they can remain hidden for decades and suddenly surface." Treating these practices as places of safety that you can use to nurture yourself and hold yourself in a compassionate reflective space as things come up can help you heal in transformative, meaningful ways. Additionally, as Dr. Cathy Cavanaugh, one of my mentors and former Chair of Wellness for Educators' Board of Directors,

Figure 4.1 Toe Squat.

said, "We can use our resistant responses as opportunities for interrogation and inquiry."

The third approach is the use of the three perceptions, including exteroception, interoception, and proprioception, all of which can support us to stay grounded in the present moment.

- **Exteroception** is how we perceive external information from our senses – sight, sound, smell, taste, and touch.
  - What are five things that I can see?
  - What are four things that I can hear?
  - What are three things that I can smell?
  - What are two things that I can taste?
  - What is one thing that I can touch?

- **Interoception** is the perception of sensations from inside the body, such as how we are able to feel our heartbeat and the air as it's moving into and out of our nose.
  - How does the air feel as I breathe in through my nose and out through my nose/mouth?
  - How does my heartbeat change as I engage in this practice?
- **Proprioception** is how we locate our body in space by way of our movement and action.
  - How is my body situated in space?
  - How does my body interact with what's around me?

Using these three perception perspectives can support us to stay in the present moment.

As you dive into the practices in the six disciplines of yoga, breathwork, meditation, mindfulness, Qigong, and yin yoga, where applicable, there are contraindications and modifications listed. Contraindications are physical conditions that may prohibit you from participating in a practice. For instance, if you have knee injuries, you may not want to engage in a practice where you're in a kneeling position, or perhaps, you can support yourself while kneeling with blankets or pillows under your knee. In cases where you are unsure if a practice is okay for you, consult your doctor before engaging in the practice.

Additionally, there are modifications offered. Modifications are alternative ways you can do a posture or practice so that you can better support yourself. For instance, if you're in a standing forward bend and your hands do not touch the floor, you can place blocks underneath your hands so that you feel as though you are touching the floor and better supporting your lower back. Another example of a modification that I just mentioned when explaining contraindications is placing pillows or blankets underneath your knees when doing a posture in a kneeling position, especially if you have knee pain.

There is also a section called "Fill Your Cup," and this area shares the qualities that each practice can support in you, such as focus, calm, and grounding.

Mind-body practices have the potential to help you heal prolonged stress and trauma from your past and present experience. As with any practice, I suggest accompanying them with a way to reflect on your experience, whether it's with a therapist, counselor, or trusted friend. You can also keep a piece of paper or a journal nearby to allow yourself to reflect on your experience. Daniel Siegel shares how narrative processes "have such powerful effects on the mind: They allow us to modulate our emotions and make sense of the world."

As previously mentioned, the research shared in this chapter is just a slice of what is available to explain the science behind these practices. It's important to note that, as educators, we put great emphasis on research-based best practices, and as a researcher, I wholeheartedly believe that research matters. At the same time, there is a tendency in academia and in the field of education in general to require the legitimizing of practices only through the lens of research, when there have been more cultural ways of legitimizing healing practices for centuries through lived experiences. Our anti-racist work is to honor these practices by including their origins. Through this intentional approach to our work, we want to honor the practices and their origins to also avoid cultural appropriation, which simply repackages what many cultures have already lived and practiced for generations for Western consumption.

I want to also acknowledge that some school staff, families, and communities may be averse to the practices shared in this book because they believe they are religious. While some of these practices did originate from philosophical underpinnings that are tied to a religion, the practices themselves are not religious. Oftentimes, when we are highly averse to something, and, perhaps, fearful of it, it's because we don't know enough about it to understand what it truly is. And sometimes our fear gets in the way of even taking the next step to learn. I invite anyone who is averse and/or fearful to explore the information in this book and elsewhere about these practices. The practices themselves support mind-body connection. I invite you to have an open mind and heart for exploration.

Yoga is up first.

CHAPTER 5

Yoga

Yoga originated between 4,000 and 5,000 years ago in India. The word *yoga* derived from the Sanskrit root *yuj* meaning "union." Put very simply, *yoga* means the union between mind and body. Most people are attracted to yoga because of the physical benefits of it, but there are many other benefits beyond that, including calmer mind, less anxiety, and better sleep, to name a few.

A study conducted by *Yoga Journal* and Yoga Alliance in 2016 reported that 36.7 million people are practicing yoga in the United States alone. There are many different styles of yoga, including but not limited to hatha, Iyengar, vinyasa, ashtanga, Bikram, Kundalini, restorative, and yin yoga. In this chapter, we focus on hatha and some restorative postures. There is a separate chapter dedicated to yin yoga because, in addition to yogic philosophy, the underpinnings of yin yoga are also aligned with Taoist philosophy.

If you're not familiar with yoga, this chapter gives you a brief introduction into some of the key concepts as well as a sampling of practices that are used to support physical, mental, social, and emotional health and wellbeing. If you're familiar with yoga, these concepts may or may not be new to you, and this chapter could serve as a good refresher. If you're not familiar with yoga, I hope you enjoy learning some key concepts about its origins and the practice.

KEY CONCEPTS

Two of the key concepts of the practice of yoga are the *eight limbs* and the *chakras*.

Eight Limbs

The eight limbs of yoga offer an understanding of how to connect the mind and body not only as we practice yoga on our mat, but also as we practice yoga in our everyday lives. This section offers a brief introduction to each of the eight limbs.

Yamas Yamas are often referred to as the social ethics of yoga. There are five Yamas: ahimsa, asteya, satya, aparigraha, and brahmacharya. While these codes typically refer to how we engage with others, there are some current interpretations that align these practices with how we engage with ourselves as well.

- Ahimsa – The practice of ahimsa is that of nonviolence. This is not only nonviolence toward others but also nonviolence toward self. In the practice of yoga on the mat, you can use ahimsa by being gentle with yourself as you learn new movements and as you learn how your body wants to move and does not want to move. For instance, as you get up and down off the floor, your ankles might make a cracking noise. Instead of getting frustrated, you can practice ahimsa by speaking kindly to yourself, expressing some self-compassion. In your everyday life off the mat, you can practice ahimsa by demonstrating compassion toward others and expressing a love for every form of life, including nature.

- Asteya – *Asteya* translates as "nonstealing." This does not have to mean in the literal sense of stealing something physical. Emma Newlyn, a 500-hour registered yoga teacher, shares that the root cause of stealing can be equated to a sense of lack, which can lead to a feeling of not being good enough, and "we begin to look for something to fill that 'empty' sensation; we often feel as though everyone else has what we want."[1] By practicing yoga, we can continue to cultivate the feeling that we are enough as we are.

- Satya – *Sat* means "being," and the practice of satya is a path to live in your truth by thinking, speaking, and acting honestly and with integrity. In yoga practice on the mat, it's a way of being with what is real within you and around you. This can also apply to our everyday life.

- Aparigraha – Nongrasping or nonattachment is a practice of letting go. There's also a translation in which *aparigraha* is "nonhoarding and generous." The shedding of "extra" could pertain to what's happening in the mind – such as societal expectations, fixed mindsets, or past experiences – to something physical in your life – such as too much clutter or toxic people or spaces. When giving up these mental and physical things, there's a freedom that can be experienced from unhealthy attachments.

- Brahmacharya – This yama is associated with the "right use of energy."[2] The practice is to focus our energy on listening to our bodies and what they need to be healthy, peaceful, and happy. This concentrated practice can be helpful on your yoga mat, but also in everyday life as you decide how to use your energy and whether that is going to serve you in a meaningful way.

Niyamas Niyamas are personal practices that help guide our lives. There are five Niyamas: santosha, soucha, swadhyaya, tapas, and ishvara pranidhana.

- Santosha – The practice of santosha is the art of working toward unconditional happiness or contentment. This progress toward contentment is not done in a striving way; rather, it is a way of being okay with what is.

- Soucha – Practicing soucha means to be pure. A useful interpretation for everyday life is to think mindfully about what we have around us and what we take in. This can be what we eat and what we take in media-wise. Anything that we digest can influence our body and mind. When we practice soucha, there's an intentionality around not only choosing what is healthy to have around you, but also choosing what is okay for you to take in through your senses.

- Swadhyaya – Sanskrit for *self-reflection*, swadhyaya is the practice of self-study. Traditionally, the practice is the studying of yogic philosophy, but modern-day practice is reflecting on who we are as well as our thoughts and actions. It's the practice of deeply connecting with ourselves not just on the mat but also as we experience life.

- Tapas – Put simply, *tapas* translates to "discipline." If we go back to the Yama asteya and the idea of not good enough, when we think about tapas, the idea of disciplining is not pushing ourselves beyond the limits and ignoring our needs. Instead, tapas is the idea of meditating every day but maybe not 30 minutes every day. Maybe today you can fit in five minutes, and that is okay. That is tapas.

- Ishvara Pranidhana – There are many meanings and translations for *ishvara pranidhana*; the one that resonates most with me is that of surrendering to the true self. Oftentimes, we work against what we need. For instance, when we're running on empty and our bodies are telling us to slow down, we often continue to push through. Ishvara pranidhana reminds us to listen to the body to hear what it's telling us and take action to fulfill its needs. Though the tides are shifting, our society sees slowing down as a sign of weakness. To choose to know your true self and take care of yourself so that you can be there more fully for others is an act of courage and bravery.

Asana Asana is what most people associate when they think of yoga. Asana is the practice of yoga postures. While it's the physical side of yoga, there is also a mental side. In yoga philosophy, it is important to take your time to reflect in each posture as well as in "the in-between" as you move from posture to posture because there is joy in the learnings for the mind as you practice as well. This slow approach also helps prevent injury.

Pranayama We're not going to spend too much time on pranayama because the next chapter is devoted to this practice. What is pranayama? *Pranayama* is translated to "breath control" but I see it more as using the breath to support the nervous system.

Pratyahara   The practice of pratyahara is one that is essential to us as educators. We get bombarded with input from every stakeholder, including our students, colleagues, leaders at the school and district levels, parents and caregivers, community members, policy makers, and more. Pratyahara is the practice of withdrawing the senses and can be likened to boundary setting. In this practice, we shut out all stimuli in order to go inward to maintain our mental health and wellbeing. By giving ourselves occasional and intentional space away from the stimuli, we make space for ourselves.

Dharana   Sanskrit for *concentration*, dharana is pointed focus typically used in the practice of meditation. Some practices of meditation focus on an object, such as a candle. Concentrating on one object can help us simplify and not get distracted.

Dhyana   Dhyana is the practice of meditation. Because there is a whole chapter dedicated to meditation, I will not spend too much time on it here. Meditation is a state of mind rather than the act of meditating itself. Meditation is the art of being fully present in the moment. As you will learn in Chapter 7 that is dedicated to meditation, there are many forms of meditation, so you can find the one(s) that work best for you.

Samadhi   *Samadhi* translates to "enlightenment," and in everyday life, samadhi is the ability to stay in the present moment. It's the ability to not be stuck wishing for the past or pining for the future.

Chakras

When people want to make fun of yoga, they often bring up the chakras (for pronunciation, think "chalk-ra" rather than "shaw-kra"). However "woo" they seem, there is science behind the chakras. Chakras are energy centers within the body where trauma and prolonged stress can get stored. There are seven chakras, and they are each associated with a part of ourselves that is vital for our day-to-day lives as human beings.

Figure 5.1 Chakras.

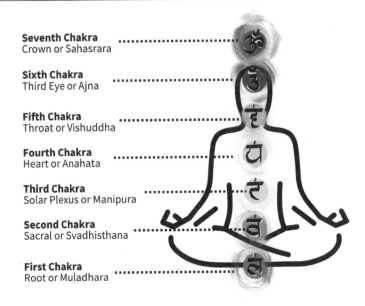

Seventh Chakra
Crown or Sahasrara

Sixth Chakra
Third Eye or Ajna

Fifth Chakra
Throat or Vishuddha

Fourth Chakra
Heart or Anahata

Third Chakra
Solar Plexus or Manipura

Second Chakra
Sacral or Svadhisthana

First Chakra
Root or Muladhara

As you do postures and meditations within yoga, you can use the chakras as a guide for creating a practice that aligns with what part of yourself needs healing. The following descriptions are not extensive. If you're interested in the chakras and what each signifies more than what is shared in the descriptions, there are plenty of websites and books with more information.

First Chakra: Root The first chakra is the root chakra, which is also known as muladhara and is located at the base of the spine. When your root chakra is balanced, you feel secure and stable. If you're struggling to feel safe and grounded, spend time in practices aligned with the root chakra.

Second Chakra: Sacral The second chakra is the sacral chakra, which is also known as svadhisthana and is located below your navel. When your sacral chakra is balanced, you feel creative and joyful. If you're struggling to feel connected and inspired, spend time in practices aligned with the sacral chakra.

Third Chakra: Solar Plexus   The third chakra is the solar plexus chakra, which is also known as manipura and is located above the navel. When your solar plexus chakra is balanced, you're confident in your abilities and personal power. If you're struggling with identity and vitality, spend time in practices aligned with the solar plexus chakra.

Fourth Chakra: Heart   The fourth chakra is the heart chakra, which is also known as anahata, and is located above the navel. When your heart chakra is balanced, you have the ability to love yourself and have compassion toward yourself and others. If you're struggling with worthiness and alienation, spend time in practices aligned with the heart chakra.

Fifth Chakra: Throat   The fifth chakra is the throat chakra, which is also known as vishuddha and is located at the throat. When your throat chakra is balanced, you can voice your beliefs and needs clearly to yourself and others. If you're struggling with communicating and confidence in speaking up for yourself and what you believe in, spend time in practices aligned with the throat chakra.

Sixth Chakra: Third Eye   The sixth chakra is the third eye, which is also known as ajna and is located in between your eyebrows. When your third eye is balanced, you have clear vision for what you want and need. If you're struggling with trusting your vision or staying focused and clear, spend time in practices aligned with the third eye chakra.

Seventh Chakra: Crown   The seventh chakra is the crown chakra, which is also known as sahasrara and is located at the top of the head. When your crown chakra is balanced, you have a clear connection to the greater good. If you're struggling with a disconnection from the world around you, spend time in practices aligned with the crown chakra.

PRACTICES

Now that you've learned a bit about yoga, it's time to practice. Before we jump in, let's revisit some key points from the "Preparation for the Practices" section of Chapter 4 so that you can be intentional about your mind-body connection as you practice yoga. This intentionality can help you reap all the benefits that result from the integration of your mind and your body.

As you engage in each posture, ask yourself the following:

- What do I notice (in my body and/or mind)? (observe without judgment)
- What do I need in this moment? (observe without judgment and give yourself what you need to feel supported)

Revisit Deb Dana's four Rs:

1. **Recognize the autonomic state.** (How is my nervous system doing? Am I in flight/fight/freeze/fawn?)

2. **Respect the adaptive survival response.** (How am I reacting? Am I crying, shaking, feeling anxious? Whatever it is, I respect the response, as it is what my nervous system needs at this time. I am not judging it.)

3. **Regulate or co-regulate into a ventral vagal state.** (What does my body and mind need now to feel safe? Do I need to hug myself? Do I need to lie down with my head on a pillow? Do I need a blanket to cover myself?)

4. **Re-story** (How can I re-frame my experience to see the learning that came up for me? What am I telling myself?)

Use the three perceptions to check in and stay grounded in the present moment:

- **Exteroception** – how we perceive external information from our senses – sight, sound, smell, taste, and touch.

- What are five things that I can see?
- What are four things that I can hear?
- What are three things that I can smell?
- What are two things that I can taste?
- What is one thing that I can touch?

- **Interoception** – how we perceive sensations from inside the body, such as how we are able to feel our heartbeat and the air as it's moving into and out of our nose.

  - How does the air feel as I breathe in through my nose and out through my nose/mouth?
  - How does my heartbeat change as I engage in this practice?

- **Proprioception** – how we perceive our body in space by way of our movement and action.

  - How is my body situated in space?
  - How does my body interact with what's around me?

As with any practice, if you're new to it, please check with your doctor to make sure this activity is conducive to your wellbeing. Also, prior to practicing, please note any modifications and contraindications that are listed with each posture.

Sun Salutation

Sun Salutation is a sequence of 12 postures that are typically practiced in the morning as a salute to a new day or salute to the sun, as the name of the practice conveys. As you are in each posture, take five breaths, and take your time in transitioning. The Sun Salutation image shares the full sequence of postures. For accessibility purposes, this series can be done with the support of a chair or wall. Each posture can also be visualized if mobility is not available.

Figure 5.2 Sun Salutation.

Mountain

Figure 5.3 Mountain.

FILL YOUR CUP

Mountain has the potential to cultivate focus, grounding, intention, presence, stability, strength, and vision.

Instructions:

- Stand with your feet together or hips-width distance apart.
- Spread your weight evenly lengthwise and widthwise through your feet.
- Make the body long from the feet to the top of the head.
- Nod head slightly forward to lengthen the back of the neck and tuck the chin slightly.
- Place your arms slightly away from the body and by your sides.
- Take five breaths.

Visit the Wellness Library to engage with this practice via video and audio:
https://well4edu.org/w4e/mountain-pose

Upward Salute

Figure 5.4 Upward Salute.

FILL YOUR CUP

Upward Salute is expansive and has the potential to cultivate energy, openness, perspective, and transformation.

Instructions:

- From Mountain, on an inhale, bring your hands up overhead.
- Take five breaths.

Standing Forward Bend

Figure 5.5 Standing Forward Bend.

FILL YOUR CUP

Standing Forward Bend has the potential to cultivate creativity, letting go, perspective, release, surrender, and transformation.

Contraindications: Back injuries

Instructions:

- From Upward Salute, on an exhale, bend at the hips.
- Lower your torso over your legs.
- Place hands somewhere along the legs, feet, or on the floor.
- Bend the knees so you do not hyperextend.
- Allow your head, neck, and shoulders to relax down.
- Take five breaths.

> Visit the Wellness Library to engage with this practice via video and audio:
> https://well4edu.org/w4e/standing-forward-bend

High Lunge

Figure 5.6 High Lunge.

FILL YOUR CUP

High Lunge has the potential to cultivate balance, focus, stability, and strength.

Contraindications: Knee issues

Instructions:

- From Standing Forward Bend, on an exhale, bend your knees.
- Place your hands on either side of your feet.
- Step your left foot back.
- Stay on the ball of the left foot.
- Take five breaths.

Modifications: Bring knee to floor.

Visit the Wellness Library to engage with this practice via video and audio:
https://well4edu.org/w4e/high-lunge

Plank

Figure 5.7 Plank.

FILL YOUR CUP

Plank has the potential to cultivate balance, focus, patience, stability, and strength.

Contraindications: Wrist issues

Instructions:

- From High Lunge, on an exhale, step your right foot back to meet the left.
- Keep your hips in line with your shoulders, knees, and ankles, not allowing the hips to drop.
- Stay on the balls of your feet as if you're in an upward position of a push-up.
- Take five breaths.

Modifications: Bring knees to floor; can be done with bent elbows and forearms on the floor.

> Visit the Wellness Library to engage with this practice via video and audio:
>
> https://well4edu.org/w4e/plank

Chaturanga

Figure 5.8 Chaturanga.

FILL YOUR CUP

Chaturanga has the potential to cultivate expansion, focus, and strength.

Instructions:

- From Plank, on an exhale, bend the elbows to 90-degree angles, keeping the elbows close to the ribs.
- Lower yourself to the floor.
- Take five breaths.

Modifications: Bring knees to floor.

Visit the Wellness Library to engage with this practice via video and audio:
 https://well4edu.org/w4e/chaturanga

Cobra

Figure 5.9 Cobra.

FILL YOUR CUP

Like Chaturanga, Cobra has the potential to cultivate expansion, focus, and strength, as well as openness and letting go.

Contraindications: Back injuries; wrist injuries; carpal tunnel syndrome; pregnancy

Instructions:

- From Chaturanga, on an inhale, make sure palms of the hands are directly underneath your shoulders.
- Using the strength of your lower back, lift your upper body from the floor.
- Take five breaths.

Modifications: Practice standing at a wall

> Visit the Wellness Library to engage with this practice via video and audio:
>   https://well4edu.org/w4e/cobra

Downward Dog

Figure 5.10 Downward Dog.

FILL YOUR CUP

Downward Dog has the potential to cultivate balance, creativity, letting go, perspective, release, and surrender.

Contraindications: High blood pressure; carpal tunnel syndrome; pregnancy

Instructions:

- From Cobra, on an exhale, lower yourself to the floor.
- Tuck your toes under.
- Make sure your hands are shoulder distance apart.
- Engage your abdominal muscles as you lift your hips into the air.
- Take five breaths.

Modifications: From Cobra, come to a tabletop position (hands and knees on all fours with flat back) and lift into an upside-down *V* position; bend knees as much as you need to.

Visit the Wellness Library to engage with this practice via video and audio:
  https://well4edu.org/w4e/downward-dog

High Lunge

Figure 5.11 High Lunge.

FILL YOUR CUP

High Lunge has the potential to cultivate balance, focus, grounding, stability, and strength.

Instructions:

- From Downward Dog, on an exhale, step your left foot forward in between your hands.

- Bend your knee to 90 degrees.
- Take five breaths.

Modifications: Bring right knee to the floor.

Visit the Wellness Library to engage with this practice via video and audio:
https://well4edu.org/w4e/high-lunge

Standing Forward Bend

Figure 5.12 Standing Forward Bend.

FILL YOUR CUP

Standing Forward Bend has the potential to cultivate creativity, letting go, perspective, release, surrender, and transformation.

Instructions:

- From High Lunge, on an exhale, step the right foot forward to meet your left foot.
- Bend at the hips.
- Lower your torso over your legs.
- Place hands somewhere along the legs, feet, or on the floor.
- Bend the knees so you do not hyperextend.
- Take five breaths.

Visit the Wellness Library to engage with this practice via video and audio:
  https://well4edu.org/w4e/standing-forward-bend

Upward Salute

Figure 5.13 Upward Salute.

FILL YOUR CUP

Upward Salute is expansive and has the potential to cultivate energy, openness, perspective, and transformation.

Instructions:

- From Standing Forward Bend, on an inhale, hinge at the hips and straighten the back.
- Slowly rise to a standing position.
- Bring your hands up overhead.
- Take five breaths.

Visit the Wellness Library to engage with this practice via video and audio:
https://well4edu.org/w4e/upward-salute

Mountain

Figure 5.14 Mountain.

FILL YOUR CUP

Mountain has the potential to cultivate focus, grounding, intention, presence, stability, strength, and vision.

Instructions:

- From Upward Salute, on an exhale, gently lower the hands down by your sides.
- Stand with your feet together or hips-width distance apart.
- Spread your weight evenly lengthwise and widthwise through your feet.
- Make the body long from the feet to the top of the head.
- Nod head slightly forward to lengthen the back of the neck and tuck the chin slightly.
- Take five breaths.

Visit the Wellness Library to engage with this practice via video and audio:
https://well4edu.org/w4e/mountain-pose

Congratulations! You've completed one-half of a round of Sun Salutation. The next time you go through it, lead with the right foot instead of the left. Once you complete that sequence, you will be done with one full round of Sun Salutation. Now that we've done a series practice, let's explore some stand-alone postures.

The Warriors

FILL YOUR CUP

There are three Warrior postures in yoga. These postures have the potential to cultivate balance, focus, grounding, stability, and strength.

Warrior I

Figure 5.15 Warrior I.

Contraindications: High blood pressure; heart problems

Instructions:

- Stand with your feet hips-width distance apart.
- Place your hands on your hips.
- Bend your knees and step the right foot back about three to four feet, making sure that your heels are hips-width distance apart.
- Bend the left knee to 90 degrees.
- Arms can be raised up overhead with hands separate or hands touching.
- Take five breaths.
- Repeat with left foot back.

Modifications: Shorten distance between feet

Visit the Wellness Library to engage with this practice via video and audio:

https://well4edu.org/w4e/warrior1

Warrior II

Figure 5.16 Warrior II.

Contraindications: High blood pressure; heart problems

Instructions:

- Stand with your feet hips-width distance apart.
- Step back with your right foot about three to four feet.
- Align the front foot's heel to the back foot's arch.
- Lift arms so that they are in line with your legs, palms facing down.
- Bend your left knee to 90 degrees, making sure not to move your knee beyond your left heel.

- Gaze over your front hand.
- Take five breaths.
- Bring feet back together.
- Repeat with left foot back.

Modifications: Shorten distance between feet

Visit the Wellness Library to engage with this practice via video and audio:
https://well4edu.org/w4e/warrior2

Warrior III

Figure 5.17 Warrior III.

Contraindications: Risk of falling; high blood pressure; heart problems

Instructions:

- Stand with your feet hips-width distance apart.
- Place your hands on your hips.
- Bend your knees and step the right foot back about three to four feet, landing on separate tracks with heels hips-width distance apart.
- Bend the left knee as you lift the right leg up behind you as you play with your balance while working toward your upper body being parallel to the floor.
- Arms can be raised up overhead with hands separate or hands touching or by the sides of your ribs.
- Take five breaths.
- Gently lower the right foot down to the floor as you bring your upper body back to standing.
- Repeat with left foot back.

Modifications: Hold onto a chair or wall

Visit the Wellness Library to engage with this practice via video and audio:
https://well4edu.org/w4e/warrior3

Balance Postures

FILL YOUR CUP

Balancing postures have the potential to cultivate balance, confidence, creativity, focus, intention, patience, presence, strength, trust, and vision.

Eagle

Figure 5.18 Eagle.

Contraindications: Knee injuries

Instructions:

- Stand with your feet hips-width distance apart.
- Bend your knees slightly.
- Begin to lift your left foot off the ground.
- Feel the weight in the right leg.
- Point your left toes and cross your left leg over your right leg. Toes can rest on the ground or be a bit off the ground.
- Stay here for your balance or take your left arm under your right arm and begin to bring your left hand to your right hand or wrist.

- Balance on the right foot.
- Take five breaths.
- Repeat with the right side.

Modifications: Keep foot on the ground

Visit the Wellness Library to engage with this practice via video and audio:
https://well4edu.org/w4e/eagle

Tree

Figure 5.19 Tree.

Contraindications: Knee pain, knee injuries (especially knee ligament injuries), or knee arthritis; shoulder pain, numbness, tingling or shooting pain when you lift your arm; risk of falling

Instructions:

- Stand with your feet hips-width distance apart.
- Bend the right knee and place the right foot on the left ankle, left calf muscle, or the left thigh. *Avoid putting your foot directly on your knee joint.*
- Place your hands on your hips.
- Make sure the standing foot continues to point straight forward and press the right foot and the left inner thigh against each other.
- Keeping the pelvis squared forward, draw the right knee back to the extent you can keep the hips square.
- To achieve greater stability and balance, find a single place of focus on which to hold your gaze, at eye level in front of you.
- Raise the arms without flaring the front ribs.
- Open the arms out to act like a tree.
- Take five breaths.
- Release your foot down.
- Shake out the standing leg and foot.
- Set up for the left side.

Modifications: Keep your hands on your hips; hold onto a chair or wall

> Visit the Wellness Library to engage with this practice via video and audio:
> https://well4edu.org/w4e/tree

Restorative Postures

Restorative yoga is a style of yoga that can help give your nervous system a reset. This yoga style allows for slow and gentle practice. Each posture is typically held for five to twenty minutes.

Legs Up the Wall

Figure 5.20 Legs Up the Wall.

FILL YOUR CUP

Legs Up the Wall has the potential to cultivate expansion, grounding, letting go, openness, perspective, restoration, surrender, transformation, and trust.

Contraindications: Eye conditions, such as glaucoma and detached retina; hernias and heart conditions; menstruation; serious neck or back issues

Instructions:

- Place a folded blanket near a wall.
- Move the hips as close to the wall as possible.

- Walk the feet up the wall until the body is in an almost L-shaped position.
- Practice long, slow breaths.
- Stay in the posture for 5 to 10 minutes.
- To come out of the posture, bring your feet to the wall and push yourself away from the wall until your legs are straight and slowly push yourself up. If you're not able to push yourself away from the wall, slowly lower the legs either to the left or the right and gently maneuver yourself away from the wall until you can safely and comfortably come up to sitting.

Modifications: Thin pillow or blanket under the head

Visit the Wellness Library to engage with this practice via video and audio:
   https://well4edu.org/w4e/legs-up-the-wall

Supported Child

Figure 5.21 Supported Child.

FILL YOUR CUP

Supported Child has the potential to cultivate calm, connection, grounding, letting go, presence, release, restoration, surrender, and trust.

Contraindications: Knee issues

Instructions:

- Begin by sitting on your heels.
- Place a bolster on the floor in front of your knees.
- Slowly fold forward, bringing your chest to the bolster.
- Place the arms alongside the body.
- Practice long, slow breaths.
- Stay in the posture for 5 to 20 minutes.
- To come out of the posture, use your hands to push the floor away and slowly roll up.

Modifications: Place a blanket between calves and glutes; use a bolster in between your legs to lift your lower body up more from the floor

Visit the Wellness Library to engage with this practice via video and audio:

https://well4edu.org/w4e/supported-childs-pose

Heart Opening

Figure 5.22 Heart Opening.

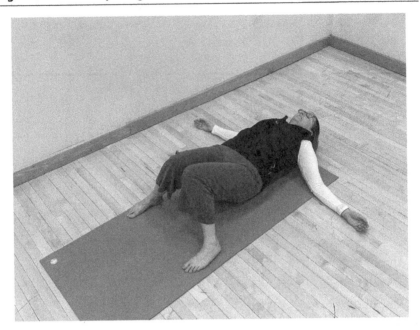

FILL YOUR CUP

Heart Opening has the potential to cultivate compassion, connection, expansion, forgiveness, heart-centeredness, openness, and restoration.

Instructions:

- Bring a bolster behind you so that the back of your hips line up with the bottom edge of the bolster.
- Rest your spine down along the bolster vertically.
- Put the soles of your feet together and open your knees out to the sides of the mat.
- Place an eye pillow or a cloth/towel over your eyes if it's comfortable for you.

- Let your hands rest either on your belly or out to the sides.
- Cover yourself with a blanket.
- Practice long, slow breaths.
- Stay here for 5 to 20 minutes.
- To come out, gently roll to one side off the bolster and press into your hands to come up.

Modifications: Place additional blankets or blocks under the outer thighs and knees if your knees or inner thighs are uncomfortable; support the head with a folded blanket on top of the bolster and under the neck

Visit the Wellness Library to engage with this practice via video and audio:

https://well4edu.org/w4e/heart-opening

Yoga Nidra

Figure 5.23 Yoga nidra nest.

Figure 5.24 Yoga nidra.

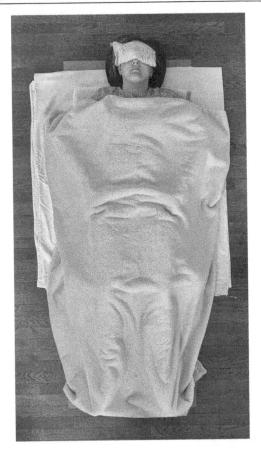

FILL YOUR CUP

Yoga nidra has the potential to cultivate balance, calm, clarity, energy, expansion, focus, grounding, letting go, openness, release, restoration, stability, and vitality.

Yoga nidra is an ancient practice that originated in India. Yoga nidra is also referred to as "yogic sleep" and is practiced for 30 to 60 minutes lying on the back in a comfortable "nest," which can include pillows, blankets, eye pillows, and so on. Personally, I like to use a travel pillow underneath my neck, extra blankets underneath my lower back/sacrum, as well as a pillow or bolster underneath my knees. When done traditionally, the practice has specific steps, including preparation, Sankalpa (intention), rotation of consciousness, breath awareness, opposite feelings and sensations, visualization, sankalpa, and ending. Sixty minutes of practice has been said to equate to four hours of sleep. Like other yoga practices, yoga nidra has been found to support the reduction of anxiety among many other mind-body benefits (Pandi-Perumal et al. 2022). Each of the steps is demonstrated through the sample script, and you can see an example of a nest as well as a practitioner in the pictures within this section.

Prepare for Practice Now that you've prepared your nest, slowly come to rest on your back, nestled in your nest.

Move as much as you need to in order to prepare your body for complete relaxation.

If you're feeling tense in any part of your body, take a bit of time to contract your muscles for 10 seconds in those areas and then release.

Do that as much as you need to until you feel completely relaxed.

Move any part of your body that does not feel 100% comfortable.

During your practice of yoga nidra, you will want to be completely relaxed and comfortable so that you don't feel like you have to move.

Once you feel comfortable, take time to scan the body from head to toe, inviting your body to relax.

Starting with the head, feeling relaxed.

Facial muscles, feeling completely relaxed.

Your upper torso and abdomen, relaxing from the inside out.

The upper and lower back, feeling relaxed.

Your upper legs and knees, completely relaxing.

Your lower legs and feet, all the way to your toes, feeling relaxed.

Feeling complete relaxation throughout your body from your head to your toes.

Choose Your Sankalpa   Now that your body is completely relaxed, invite yourself to create a Sankalpa, an intention, something that you would like to cultivate in your life.

I am peace. I am health. I am love. I am contentment. I am power.

Whatever resonates with you in this moment is your intention. Take a few moments to set your intention for your practice.

Once you have set your intention, say your intention three times to yourself, allowing it to settle in your mind and travel between the mind and your heart center.

With every breath in, cultivating that seed, that intention.

With every breath out, clearing out anything that gets in the way of that intention.

Rotate Consciousness   Now that you've set your intention, you're going to take your awareness on a mindful journey through your body from one point to the next.

As you journey through your body from point to point, do not linger on any one point.

Just continue to move from point to point without attachment to any one point.

The thumb of your right hand

Pointer finger

Middle finger

Ring finger

Pinky finger

The palm of your hand

The back of your hand

Your wrist

Forearm

Elbow

Upper arm

Shoulder

The right side body

Your waist

Hip

Thigh

Knee

Calf

Shin

Ankle

The heel of your foot

The sole of your foot

Your right big toe

2nd toe

3rd toe

4th toe

5th toe

The whole right side of the body

Bringing your awareness to the whole right side of the body

Your right side body

Continuing your journey to the left side body

The thumb of your left hand

Pointer finger

Middle finger

Ring finger

Pinky finger

The palm of your hand

The back of your hand

Your wrist

Forearm

Elbow

Upper arm

Shoulder

The left side body

Your waist

Hip

Thigh

Knee

Calf

Shin

Ankle

The heel of your foot

The sole of your foot

Your left big toe

2nd toe

3rd toe

4th toe

5th toe

The whole left side of the body

Bringing your awareness to the whole left side of the body

Your left side body

Continuing your journey to the back body

Back of your head

Back of your neck

The whole back, both left back and right back

Right shoulder blade

Left shoulder blade

The whole lower back, both left lower back and right lower back

The whole back body

Bringing your awareness to the whole back body

Your whole back body

Continuing your journey to the front body

Your abdomen

Your chest

Throat

Chin

Lips, upper and lower

Cheeks, both left and right

Nose

Ears, both left and right

Eyes, both left and right

Your forehead

The top of your head

The whole front body

Bringing your awareness to the whole front body

Your whole front body

Bringing your awareness to your whole body

Mindfully bringing your attention to every part of your body as you sweep
   your awareness from the top of your head to the tips of your toes

Bringing your awareness to your whole body, relaxing your whole body

Be Aware of Your Breath Continuing the journey of relaxation with awareness, move to your breath. Mentally visualizing your breath as it travels in through your nose and out through your nose.

With each breath in, continuing to feel your breath fill you with vital air.

With each breath out, continuing to relax the mind and body.

As you watch your breath travel through your nose, in and out, begin to count backwards from 54.

Breathing in 54, breathing out 54.

Breathing in 53, breathing out 53.

Breathing in 52, breathing out 52.

And continuing to count, naturally following your own breath's pace and pattern.

If you complete your count to 1, start over.

If you become distracted or lose count, start over without judgment.

[Pause for 2 minutes to allow for internal counting.]

Feel and Sense Opposites Your journey now flows into feeling and sensing opposites. Starting with cold.

Welcome the feeling of cold in your body.

Feeling cold within your body from your head to your feet.

Coolness permeating your toes, up your legs, into the trunk of your body, and up to the crown of the head.

Feeling cool throughout your whole body.

Cold throughout your body.

Filling yourself with heat now.

Welcome the feeling of heat into your body.

Feeling hot within your body from your head to your feet.

Heat permeating your toes, up your legs, into the trunk of your body, and up to the crown of the head.

Feeling heat through your whole body.

Hot throughout your body.

Visualize As part of your journey, you set off on an adventure to the Emerald Forest.

This journey that you are on will bring you to a guide, someone from your past, present, or future who can provide you guidance for something you've been thinking about.

As you set off on a dirt path, the temperature is not too cold, not too warm.

The path is set between two fields of tall grass.

The breeze blows the grass, making the grass look like waves in a green ocean.

The path meanders left and right, up and down small rolling hills.

You watch as different birds fly in the blue sky, swooping around, calling to each other.

You see white clouds slowly moving their way across the sky.

You smell the grass and begin to see the pine trees in the distance.

As you continue to walk the path, the pine trees grow taller and taller before you.

You reach the first rows of pine trees.

You've arrived at the Emerald Forest.

As you enter the forest, the air cools and dampens.

You pull a sweatshirt on that you've been carrying.

You continue to venture into the woods.

The forest's canopy allows streaks of light in from the sun, which is now directly overhead.

The path is filled with twigs, branches, leaves, and moss.

You see squirrels and chipmunks foraging on the ground and running up the trees.

As the path turns to the right, you notice a bit of a clearing before you.

The clearing is the center of the forest.

At the clearing, there is a small pond.

As you reach the pond, you look in.

In the pond, there are rocks and green vegetation.

Lily pads at the top of the water act as springboards for the frogs that jump from one to another and into the pond to swim.

You also notice your reflection in the water.

As you look into the water, you can also see your guide.

Your guide can be a trusted friend, an animal, someone from the past or present who can offer you support.

Take a few minutes to ask your friend for guidance and listen to the message that they have to share with you. Also tell your friend your intention, saying it three times clearly.

[Pause for 2 minutes.]

Thank your friend for listening to you and for providing you with guidance.

Thank yourself for taking time to be with your friend and for asking for support.

You find a comfortable spot on the ground or near the pond to lie down to rest.

Take time to rest for the next several minutes.

You'll hear my voice again after your rest.

Rest gently until then.

[Pause for 10 minutes.]

Arising from your resting place in the forest, you turn to face the path that leads you back to where you started your journey.

You continue walking the path, through the forest.

You reach the edge of the forest and see the grassy fields to the left and right of the dirt path.

As the sun is starting to slowly come down in the sky, you can tell it's a couple of hours before sunset.

You enjoy the peacefulness of the wind in the grass, the clouds in the sky, and the sun's warmth.

When you reach the point where you started, you lie down in a field of tall grass as the sun begins to set, resting a bit from your journey to the Emerald Forest.

[Pause for 2 minutes.]

Revisit Your Sankalpa   Breathing in, cultivating your intention.

Breathing out, letting go of anything that is in the way of your intention.

End Your Practice   Breathing in, feeling the breath flowing into the body.

Breathing out, feeling the breath flowing out of the body.

Bringing awareness to the feeling of the breath as it flows into and out of your body as you breathe in and breathe out.

Yoga nidra is now complete.

Continuing to breathe in and out as you bring your attention to your mind and body.

When you're ready, gently wiggle the fingers and the toes, rotate the wrists and ankles.

If it feels okay, bring your knees into your chest and gently rock from side to side.

When you're ready, bring yourself up to a seated position.

Bowing the head toward the heart center as you bring one hand over the heart and the other hand over that hand.

Thanking yourself for practicing yoga nidra, for taking the time and making the space that you need to take care of yourself.

Fill your own cup first so you can fill the cups of others.

Visit the Wellness Library to engage with this practice via video and audio:

https://well4edu.org/w4e/yoga-nidra

There are many more postures and practices in yoga that you can explore with the help of a certified yoga instructor. We're going to move onto breathwork in the next chapter.

ADDITIONAL RESOURCES

If you'd like to learn more about the practice of yoga, I've included some resources. There are plenty more resources; these are the ones I personally recommend to others and go back to as references.

Books

Dianne Bondy – *Yoga for Everyone: 50 Poses for Every Type of Body*
Judith Hanson Lasater – *Relax and Renew: Restful Yoga for Stressful Times*
B.K.S. Iyengar – *Light on Yoga*

Dr. Gail Parker
- *Restorative Yoga for Ethnic and Race-Based Stress and Trauma*
- *Transforming Ethnic and Race-Based Traumatic Stress with Yoga*

Dr. Arielle Schwartz – *Therapeutic Yoga for Trauma Recovery*

Jessamyn Stanley – *Every Body Yoga*

Websites/Social Media

Black Boys Om
https://www.instagram.com/blackboysom
Kripalu Center for Yoga & Health
https://kripalu.org/
Jennifer Reis – Divine Sleep Yoga https://jenniferreisyoga.com/divine-sleep-yoga-nidra/divine-sleep-yoga-nidra-teacher-training/
Sagel Urlacher – Yoga Nidra
https://www.yinandmeditation.com/teacher-trainings/yoga-nidra
Wellness for Educators – Wellness Library
http://well4edu.org/wellness-library

NOTES

1. Emma Newlyn. "The Yamas: Asteya – non-stealing." https://www.ekhartyoga.com/articles/philosophy/the-yamas-asteya-non-stealing.
2. Emma Newlyn. "The Yamas: Brahmacharya, right use of energy." https://www.ekhartyoga.com/articles/philosophy/the-yamas-brahmacharya-right-use-of-energy.

CHAPTER 6

Breathwork

As is mentioned in the last chapter, breathwork is one of the eight limbs of yoga. It is known as pranayama. While *pranayama* translates to "the control of the breath," the practice of pranayama is really about using the breath as a way to support the nervous system and ready the body for meditation. In yoga, we start with asana to prepare the body and mind for meditation, then breathwork to further prepare the mind, and then we meditate. Breathwork is known to be one of the best exercises to stimulate the vagus nerve, which calms the nervous system. It is also important to note that breathing is an essential part of asana (physical postures), but these practices have a pointed effect on the mind. In this chapter, we'll briefly explore some of the key concepts of pranayama and then spend time with some of the practices.

KEY CONCEPTS

The key concepts of breathwork are inhalation and exhalation, as well as internal and external retention.

- Inhalation – Also known as *puraka*, inhalation is done through the nose.
- Exhalation – Often referred to as *rechaka*, exhalation is typically done through the nose, but in some practices, such as Breath of Joy and Lion's Breath, it's done through the nose and the mouth.
- Retention – Breath retention, also called *khumbaka*, can be done while holding the breath in (*antara-khumbaka*) as well as when holding the breath out (*bahya-khumbaka*).

Now that we have the key concepts, let's jump into the practices!

PRACTICES

Now that you've learned a bit about breathwork, it's time to practice. Note that, as a beginner, some of these breathing practices may induce an intense response. For instance, doing the Three-Part Breath, which is a really long breath, was really hard for me at first and made me feel anxious. Rather than forcing myself to stay with the breath when I experienced the anxiety, I practiced self-compassion and came back to the practice when I was ready. You can do the same thing. Remember to continuously check in to see how you're feeling and make changes to your practice according to your needs.

Before we jump in, let's revisit some key points from the "Preparation for the Practices" section of Chapter 4 so that we can be intentional about the mind-body connection as we practice breathwork. This intentionality can help us reap all the benefits that result from the integration of the mind and the body.

As you engage in each pranayama practice, ask yourself the following:

- What do I notice (in my body and/or mind)? (observe without judgment)
- What do I need in this moment? (observe without judgment and give yourself what you need to feel supported)

Revisit Deb Dana's four Rs:

1. **Recognize the autonomic state.** (How is my nervous system doing? Am I in flight/fight/freeze/fawn?)

2. **Respect the adaptive survival response.** (How am I reacting? Am I crying, shaking, feeling anxious? Whatever it is, I respect the response, as it is what my nervous system needs. I am not judging it.)

3. **Regulate or co-regulate into a ventral vagal state.** (What does my body and mind need now to feel safe? Do I need to hug myself? Do I need to lie down with my head on a pillow? Do I need a blanket to cover myself?)

4. **Re-story** (How can I re-frame my experience to see the learning that came up for me? What am I telling myself?)

Use the three perceptions to check in and stay grounded in the present moment:

- **Exteroception** – how we perceive external information from our senses – sight, sound, smell, taste, and touch.
  - What are five things that I can see?
  - What are four things that I can hear?
  - What are three things that I can smell?
  - What are two things that I can taste?
  - What is one thing that I can touch?
- **Interoception** – how we perceive sensations from inside the body, such as how we can feel our heartbeat and the air as it's moving into and out of our nose.
  - How does the air feel as I breathe in through my nose and out through my nose/mouth?
  - How does my heartbeat change as I engage in this practice?
- **Proprioception** – how we perceive our body in space by way of our movement and action.
  - How is my body situated in space?
  - How does my body interact with what's around me?

As with any practice, if you're new to it, please check with your doctor to make sure this activity is conducive to your wellbeing. Also, prior to practicing, please note any modifications and contraindications that are listed with each practice.

Three-Part Breath

Figure 6.1 Three-Part Breath.

FILL YOUR CUP

Three-Part Breath, also known as Dirgha Breath, has the potential to cultivate calm, grounding, release, restoration, and stability.

Contraindications: Asthma; other breathing conditions

Instructions:

- Lie on your back with your eyes closed, relaxing your face and your body. You can keep the legs outstretched or bend your knees and bring the soles of your feet to your mat if that's more comfortable. If you bend your knees, let them rest against each other.

- Begin by observing the natural inhalation and exhalation of your breath without changing anything.

- Part One:
  - Begin to inhale and exhale deeply through the nose.
  - On each inhale, fill the belly up with your breath. Expand the belly with air like a balloon.
  - On each exhale, expel all the air out from the belly through your nose. Draw your navel back toward your spine to make sure that the belly is empty of air.
  - Repeat this deep belly breathing for about five breaths.
- Part Two:
  - On the next inhale, fill the belly up with air. Then, when the belly is full, draw in a little more breath and let that air expand into the rib cage causing the ribs to widen apart.
  - On the exhale, let the air go first from the rib cage, letting the ribs slide closer together, and then from the belly, drawing the navel back toward the spine.
  - Repeat this deep breathing into the belly and rib cage for about five breaths.
- Part Three:
  - On the next inhale, fill the belly and rib cage up with air. Then sip in just a little more air and let it fill the upper chest, all the way up to the collarbone, causing the area around the heart to expand and rise.
  - On the exhale, let the breath go first from the upper chest, allowing the heart center to sink back down, then from the rib cage, letting the ribs slide closer together. Finally, let the air go from the belly, drawing the navel back toward the spine.
- Continue at your own pace, eventually letting the three parts of the breath happen smoothly without pausing.
- Continue for about 10 breaths.

Modifications: Can be practiced in a seated or standing position

Visit the Wellness Library to engage with this practice via video and audio:
    https://well4edu.org/w4e/three-part-breath

Surya Bhedana

Figure 6.2 Surya Bhedana.

FILL YOUR CUP

Surya Bhedana has the potential to cultivate clarity, confidence, courage, energy, focus, intention, presence, strength, vision, and vitality.

Contraindications: Epilepsy; heart disease; anxiety; and high blood pressure

Surya stands for "sun" and *bhedana* stands for "piercing" in Sanskrit; thus, *Surya Bhedana* is the practice of "piercing the sun." This is a warming breath that wakes up the energy in your body. I like to practice this breathing technique when I'm feeling sleepy or low energy, especially right after lunchtime.

Instructions:

- Place the right hand in Vishnu Mudra (forefinger and middle finger bent toward the palm; thumb, ring, and pinky fingers in the air).
- Close off the left nostril with the ring and pinky fingers.
- Breathe in and out of the right nostril.
- Continue doing 5–20 rounds.

Modifications: If your right nostril is stuffed up, try clearing it by blowing your nose. If your nose is still stuffed up, you can visualize the practice of inhaling and exhaling through the right nostril without closing off the left nostril.

Visit the Wellness Library to engage with this practice via video and audio:
https://well4edu.org/w4e/surya-bhedana

Chandra Bhedana

Figure 6.3 Chandra Bhedana.

FILL YOUR CUP

Chandra Bhedana has the potential to cultivate calm, compassion, heart-centeredness, letting go, release, restoration, and surrender.

Chandra stands for "moon" and *bhedana* stands for "piercing" in Sanskrit; thus, *Chandra Bhedana* is the practice of "piercing the moon." This is a cooling breath that relaxes the energy in your body. I like to practice this breathing technique when I'm having a hard time calming down before I go to sleep or if I need to relax after something riles me up or distracts me.

Instructions:

- Place the right hand in Vishnu Mudra (forefinger and middle finger bent toward the palm; thumb, ring, and pinky fingers in the air).
- Close off the right nostril with the thumb.
- Breathe in and out of the left nostril.
- Continue doing 5–20 rounds.

Modifications: If your left nostril is stuffed up, try clearing it by blowing your nose. If your nose is still stuffed up, you can visualize the practice of inhaling and exhaling through the left nostril without closing off the right nostril.

Visit the Wellness Library to engage with this practice via video and audio:

https://well4edu.org/w4e/chandra-bhedana

Nadi Shodhana

Figure 6.4 Nadi Shodhana.

FILL YOUR CUP

Nadi Shodhana has the potential to cultivate clarity, focus, calm, grounding, and letting go.

Also known as Alternate Nostril Breathing, this practice evens out the mind, and helps us to be clear and calm at the same time. It is a combination of Surya Bhedana and Chandra Bhedana to bring balance to your mind and body.

Instructions:

- Place the right hand in Vishnu Mudra (forefinger and middle finger bent toward the palm; thumb, ring, and pinky in the air).
- One round:
  - Close off the right nostril with the thumb.
  - Inhale into the left nostril.
  - Close the left nostril with the ring and pinky fingers.
  - Open the right nostril.
  - Exhale through the right nostril.
  - Inhale into the right nostril.
  - Close the right nostril.
  - Open the left nostril.
  - Exhale through the left nostril.
- Continue doing 5–20 rounds.

Visit the Wellness Library to engage with this practice via video and audio:
https://well4edu.org/w4e/alternate-nostril-breathing

Ujjayi

FILL YOUR CUP

Ujjayi, also known as Ocean Breath, has the potential to cultivate calm, focus, and presence.

Contraindications: Asthma

Instructions:

- Inhale and exhale through your mouth.
- On the next exhale, pretend you are cleaning your glasses. That is the type of sound you want to make in the back of your throat.
- When you can control the throat on both the inhale and the exhale, close the mouth and begin breathing through the nose.
- Continue for about 10 breaths.

> Visit the Wellness Library to engage with this practice via video and audio:
> https://well4edu.org/w4e/ocean-breath

Bhramari

Figure 6.5 Bhramari.

FILL YOUR CUP

Bhramari is also known as Bee's Breath. This practice has the potential to cultivate clarity, focus, grounding, letting go, and presence.

Contraindications: Best to practice on an empty stomach; Bee's Breath should not be practiced by pregnant or menstruating women. It is also contraindicated for individuals with extremely high blood pressure, epilepsy, chest pain, or an active ear infection; Bee's Breath should not be practiced in a supine position (lying down).

Instructions:

- Find a comfortable seat on the floor with a cushion or blanket to comfortably elevate the hips.
- Back is tall and the shoulders are relaxed.
- While not required, you can also place your fingers in Shanmukhi Mudra (hand position) while doing this practice. Shanmukhi Mudra: gently place your thumbs on the ear cartilage, index fingers on the forehead just above the eyebrows, middle fingers on eyes, ring fingers on either side of your nose, and the pinky fingers on the corners of your lips.
- Start by taking a few natural breaths.
- Close your eyes if you feel comfortable doing so.
- Then, keeping the lips lightly sealed, inhale through the nose.
- Exhale and make a "hmmm" sound at the back of the throat – like the humming of a bee.
- Repeat: inhale through the nose, then hum like a buzzing bee as you exhale.
- Continue by inhaling as needed and exhaling with this sound for several minutes.
- Allow your breath to return to normal and observe any changes.

Modifications: If Shanmukhi Mudra is too much and makes you feel claustrophobic, you can practice this by just closing the eyes and blocking off the ears; sit on the edge of a chair with feet flat on the floor.

Visit the Wellness Library to engage with this practice via video and audio:
   https://well4edu.org/w4e/bees-breath

Sitkari or Sitali

Figure 6.6 Sitkari.

Figure 6.7 Sitali.

FILL YOUR CUP

Sitkari or Sitali are two types of pranayama that cultivate cooling in the mind and body. They have the potential to cultivate calm, grounding, letting go, release, restoration, and surrender.

Contraindications: Low blood pressure; asthma; bronchitis; excessive mucus; chronic constipation; refrain from practicing in winter or cool climates

Instructions:

- Sitkari
  - Sit in a comfortable meditation position.
  - Close your eyes if it is comfortable for you.
  - Extend the tongue outside the mouth and roll it so that it forms a tube (hot dog bun).
  - Inhale through the rolled tongue.
  - At the end of the inhalation, draw the tongue in, close the mouth and exhale through the nose.
  - Continue for 10 breaths.
- Sitali:
  - Hold the teeth lightly together.
  - Separate the lips to expose the teeth.
  - The tongue can be kept flat or lightly touching the soft palate.
  - Inhale through the teeth.
  - At the end of the inhale, close the mouth.
  - Exhale slowly through the nose.
  - Continue for 10 breaths.

Visit the Wellness Library to engage with this practice via video and audio:
https://well4edu.org/w4e/cooling-breath

Lion's Breath

Figure 6.8 Lion's Breath – Inhale.

Figure 6.9 Lion's Breath – Exhale.

FILL YOUR CUP

Lion's Breath has the potential to cultivate calm, clarity, energy, focus, letting go, perspective, release, and vision.

Instructions:

- Begin by inhaling through the nose.
- Scrunch up all your face muscles.
- Open your mouth.
- Stick out your tongue.
- Exhale through the mouth.

- If you'd like to, make the sound of the lion's roar as you exhale.
- Continue for 8–10 breaths.

Visit the Wellness Library to engage with this practice via video and audio:
    https://well4edu.org/w4e/eye-palming-and-lions-breath

Breath of Joy

FILL YOUR CUP

Breath of Joy has the potential to cultivate energy, grounding, letting go, openness, perspective, release, surrender, and transformation.

Contraindications: Shoulder injuries; back injuries

Instructions:

- Stand with feet hip-width distance apart.
- In one continuous movement, raise your arms up in front of your body to shoulder height with palms facing down while taking a sip of air (one-third of a full breath in).
- Then move the arms out to your sides, parallel with the floor with palms facing down while taking another sip of air (another one-third of a full breath in).
- Move arms straight above your head, palms facing each other while taking another sip of air (the last one-third of a full breath in).
- Rapidly lower arms in front, bending at the hips, bending the knees.
- Exhale forcefully through an open mouth.
- Repeat 8–10 times.

Modifications: Sit in a chair; practice without bending at the hips

Visit the Wellness Library to engage with this practice via video and audio:
https://well4edu.org/w4e/breath-of-joy

I hope you've enjoyed practicing the variety of pranayama that yoga has to offer. There are others you can explore. Now, we're going to move on to the practice of meditation.

ADDITIONAL RESOURCES

If you'd like to learn more about the practice of breathwork, I've included some resources. There are plenty more resources; these are the ones I personally recommend to others and go back to as references.

Books

Donna Farhi – *The Breathing Book: Good Health and Vitality through Essential Breath Work*
Thich Nhat Hanh – *Breathe, You Are Alive!*
B.K.S. Iyengar – *Light on Pranayama: The Yogic Art of Breathing*
Jennifer Patterson – *The Power of Breathwork: Simple Practices to Promote Wellbeing*

CHAPTER 7

Meditation

The practice of meditation comes in many different forms. For the purposes of the practices section of this chapter, I briefly introduce you to several meditation disciplines so that you can explore and find the one(s) that is/are most meaningful to you. Please note that this is not an exhaustive list. Each discipline of meditation has its own concepts, so for this chapter, we'll explore each meditation discipline and its concepts, and engage in a practice. In this chapter, you learn about mantra meditation, chakra meditation, loving-kindness meditation, self-compassion meditation, walking meditation, and Zen meditation. We cover three other meditations in Chapters 8, 9, and 10, which include mindfulness meditation, Qigong meditation, and yin meditation.

KEY CONCEPTS AND PRACTICES

Before we jump in, let's revisit some key points from the "Preparation for the Practices" section of Chapter 4 so that we can be intentional about the mind-body connection as we practice each of these meditations. This intentionality can help us reap all the benefits that result from the integration of the mind and the body.

As you engage in each meditation, ask yourself the following:

- What do I notice (in my body and/or mind)? (observe without judgment)
- What do I need in this moment? (observe without judgment and give yourself what you need to feel supported)

Revisit Deb Dana's four Rs:

1. **Recognize the autonomic state.** (How is my nervous system doing? Am I in flight/fight/freeze/fawn?)

2. **Respect the adaptive survival response.** (How am I reacting? Am I crying, shaking, feeling anxious? Whatever it is, I respect the response, as it is what my nervous system needs. I am not judging it.)

3. **Regulate or co-regulate into a ventral vagal state.** (What does my body and mind need now to feel safe? Do I need to hug myself? Do I need to lie down with my head on a pillow? Do I need a blanket to cover myself?)

4. **Re-story** (How can I re-frame my experience to see the learning that came up for me? What am I telling myself?)

Use the three perceptions to check in and stay grounded in the present moment:

- **Exteroception** – how we perceive external information from our senses – sight, sound, smell, taste, and touch.
  - What are five things that I can see?
  - What are four things that I can hear?
  - What are three things that I can smell?
  - What are two things that I can taste?
  - What is one thing that I can touch?
- **Interoception** – how we perceive sensations from inside the body, such as how we can feel our heartbeat and the air as it's moving into and out of our nose.
  - How does the air feel as I breathe in through my nose and out through my nose/mouth?
  - How does my heartbeat change as I engage in this practice?
- **Proprioception** – how we perceive our body in space by way of our movement and action.
  - How is my body situated in space?
  - How does my body interact with what's around me?

As with any practice, if you're new to meditation, please check with your doctor to make sure this activity is conducive to your wellbeing.

Mantra Meditation

Using mantras as a meditation is a useful way to keep your mind focused on something. Mantras can be words, phrases, or just sounds that you can sing or hum aloud or silently repeat in your head. One common example of a mantra is the word *Aum* or *Om*, which is a mantra based in yogic tradition. Om is considered the foundational sound of the universe. If you're not comfortable using something like Om, you can choose a word or phrase or sound that resonates with you. For instance, when I am feeling anxious, I use the words "safe" on my breath in, and "calm" on my breath out. As you're deciding on a mantra that works for you and your practice, think of choosing something that will help you make a meaningful change in your life. The vibrations caused by the sound you create as you are saying your mantra can also support your nervous system. Marian Diamond, a neuroscientist from the University of California, and others have found that mantra meditation can block the release of stress hormones adrenaline and cortisol, decreasing anxiety and stress while increasing immune function (Amin et al. 2016). Once you have chosen a mantra, use the following instructions to engage in mantra meditation.

FILL YOUR CUP

Mantra meditation has the potential to cultivate grounding and presence. What you cultivate will also depend on the mantra you use.

Instructions:

- Sit comfortably in a chair or on the floor.
- Place your hands in your lap.
- Close your eyes if that's comfortable for you or have a soft gaze.
- Repeat your mantra aloud or in your mind as you inhale and as you exhale.
- Sit for 5–20 minutes.

- If you find your mind wandering, return to your mantra without judgment.
- After you finish your designated meditation time, take notice of how you feel for a minute or two.

Visit the Wellness Library to engage with this practice via video and audio:

https://well4edu.org/w4e/mantra-meditation

Chakra Meditation

If need be, take a minute to revisit the "Key Concepts" section of Chapter 5 focused on the chakras. There are many meditation practices that are dedicated to the chakras overall, but also meditations for each individual chakra. These meditations are used to help unblock stuck energy in the chakras (parts of the body). Some of these meditations are like the mantra meditations where the practices use sound healing, such as your voice. Let's try practicing a chakra meditation that supports all the chakras.

Deep Breathing Chakra Meditation

FILL YOUR CUP

Deep breathing chakra meditation has the potential to cultivate balance, clarity, connection, energy, expansion, grounding, intention, presence, stability, and vitality.

Instructions:

- Find a quiet place.
- Sit comfortably on the floor or in a chair.

- Place your hands on your legs with palms facing upward.
- Close your eyes if that's comfortable for you or have a soft gaze.
- Place your hands on your abdomen.
- Start with one deep breath in.
- As you inhale through your nose, feel your abdomen expand as you slowly count to four.
- Hold the air in your lungs for a count of four.
- Exhale the air out of your mouth for a count of four.
- Hold the air out of your lungs for a count of four.
- Continue this breath as you visualize each of the chakras.
- Visualize the root chakra at the base of your spine. You can visualize it as a red flower or whatever is most meaningful to you. Imagine it expanding as you engage your breath in and out. Do 3–5 rounds of in and out breaths while you visualize your root chakra.
- Visualize the sacral chakra right below your navel. You can visualize it as an orange flower or whatever is most meaningful to you. Imagine it expanding as you engage your breath in and out. Do 3–5 rounds of in and out breaths while you visualize your root chakra.
- Visualize the solar plexus chakra right below your navel. You can visualize it as a yellow flower or whatever is most meaningful to you. Imagine it expanding as you engage your breath in and out. Do 3–5 rounds of in and out breaths while you visualize your solar plexus chakra.
- Visualize the heart chakra, located near your heart, in the center of your chest. You can visualize it as a green flower or whatever is most meaningful to you. Imagine it expanding as you engage your breath in and out. Do 3–5 rounds of in and out breaths while you visualize your heart chakra.
- Visualize the throat chakra, located at the base of your throat. You can visualize it as a blue flower or whatever is most meaningful to you. Imagine it expanding as you engage your breath in and out. Do 3–5 rounds of in and out breaths while you visualize your throat chakra.

- Visualize the third eye chakra, located on your forehead, between your eyebrows. You can visualize it as an indigo flower or whatever is most meaningful to you. Imagine it expanding as you engage your breath in and out. Do 3–5 rounds of in and out breaths while you visualize your third eye chakra.

- Visualize the crown chakra, located at the top of your head. You can visualize it as a violet flower or whatever is most meaningful to you. Imagine it expanding as you engage your breath in and out. Do 3–5 rounds of in and out breaths while you visualize your crown chakra.

- Do another 7 rounds of in and out breaths while you visualize each of the seven chakras per each of the 7 rounds.

- Finish the meditation by taking a couple of natural breaths in and out.

> Visit the Wellness Library to engage with this practice via video and audio:
> https://well4edu.org/w4e/chakra-meditation

Loving-Kindness Meditation

Also known as metta, loving-kindness meditation is a Buddhist practice of unconditional and inclusive love. Earlier versions of loving-kindness are found in Hindu tradition as self-compassion. We'll practice that after this loving-kindness meditation. Metta is practiced not only toward others, but also toward ourselves. As you say the phrases associated with loving-kindness, let them resonate at your heart center, feeling the warmth and love that reverberates from their repetition. It also helps to visualize the person you are saying the phrases to. Note, too, that feelings might arise that are difficult, such as anger and grief. Let those feelings come up. Witness and feel them without judgment.

FILL YOUR CUP

Loving-kindness meditation has the potential to cultivate compassion, connection, forgiveness, heart-centeredness, openness, and restoration.

Instructions:

- Find a quiet space.
- Sit in a comfortable and relaxed manner either in a chair or on the floor.
- Take three deep breaths with slow, long, and complete exhalations.
- Visualize your breath coming into and out of your heart center.
- Visualize yourself in your mind.
- Repeat the following phrases to yourself three times:
  - May I be happy. May I be well. May I be safe. May I be peaceful and at ease.
- Visualize a friend or loved one who deeply loves you and cares for you.
- Repeat the following phrases toward them three times:
  - May you be happy. May you be well. May you be safe. May you be peaceful and at ease.
- Visualize someone with whom you have difficulty.
- Repeat the following phrases toward them three times:
  - May you be happy. May you be well. May you be safe. May you be peaceful and at ease.
- Visualize all beings.
- Repeat the following phrases toward all beings three times:
  - May all beings be happy. May all beings be well. May all beings be safe. May all beings be peaceful and at ease.

Visit the Wellness Library to engage with this practice via video and audio:

https://well4edu.org/w4e/loving-kindness-meditation

Self-Compassion Meditation

As Buddha said, "If your compassion does not include yourself, it is incomplete." It's easy to have compassion for others when they make mistakes. It's often hard to do the same for ourselves. Self-compassion is so important to practice, to be aware of our own suffering. Our practice for this meditation is called Calm-Hearted Self-Compassion Meditation.

Calm-Hearted Self-Compassion Meditation

FILL YOUR CUP

Calm-hearted self compassion meditation has the potential to cultivate balance, calm, compassion, grounding, heart-centeredness, openness, and restoration.

Instructions:

- Find a comfortable seated position in a chair or on the floor.
- Find a soft gaze with your eyes or allow them to close.
- Place your right hand over your heart.
- Place your left hand on your left knee.
- Bring a mistake you made into your awareness.
- As you do each of the breaths in and out, and as you retain your breath, repeat the phrase "May I forgive myself."
- Begin by inhaling for a count of 4.

- Hold the breath in for a count of 7.
- Exhale for a count of 8.
- Continue for 7 rounds.
- Return to your natural breath.
- Gently open your eyes when you're ready.

Visit the Wellness Library to engage with this practice via video and audio:

https://well4edu.org/w4e/self-compassion-meditation

Walking Meditation

Oftentimes, meditation is associated with sitting and being still. That is not always the case. You can make most movement activities a meditation practice. For instance, a friend of mine uses her knitting activity as her daily meditation. The key to meditation is to make it work for you. Walking meditation can help us connect with nature and the world around us.

FILL YOUR CUP

Walking meditation has the potential to cultivate calm, clarity, grounding, intention, patience, perspective, presence, stability, and vision.

Instructions:

- Decide on an amount of time to engage in your walking meditation.
- Start with the left foot.
- Pick up the left foot as you walk.

- Feel the foot from heel to toe as you walk.
- Switch to the right foot, heel to toe.
- Notice any internal sensations in the mind and body as you move.
- Notice any external sensations in the mind and body as you notice yourself in your surroundings.
- As thoughts come up in the mind, focus on what's happening around you to bring yourself back to the present moment.
- As you feel moved to do so, stop walking and pause for five breaths.
- Continue walking until the end of your meditation time.

Visit the Wellness Library to engage with this practice via video and audio:
https://well4edu.org/w4e/walking-meditation

Zen Meditation

Originating from Zen Buddhism over 1,000 years ago, Zen meditation is also called zazen, which is a sitting meditation. The focus for zazen is maintaining proper posture, including straight spine, relaxed abdomen, and open shoulders. Like yoga practice, the hope is that the awareness that we reach in our meditation will carry over to our everyday lives. In the practice, you concentrate on your breath in and out, one at a time, while ignoring any thoughts that come up. The practice is less focused on self and more focused on all beings.

Zazen

FILL YOUR CUP

Zazen has the potential to cultivate calm, connection, focus, and intention.

Instructions:

- Choose an amount of time you'd like to practice zazen and set a timer.
- Find a quiet space.
- Sit on the floor (kneeling or legs crossed) or in a chair with a back with feet on the floor.
- Ensure that the back and head are straight with the crown of the head pointing upward to the sky or ceiling.
- Align your ears with shoulders.
- Tuck your chin in slightly.
- Eyes should be open and lowered at a 45-degree angle but not focused on anything.
- Inhale and exhale as you rock right to left three times.
- Place hands in your lap in zazen mudra (left hand resting on right hand with palms facing up and tips of thumbs lightly touching).
- Focus on your breath, in and out through the nose in a natural manner.
- Breath in, count 1.
- Breath out, count 2.
- Breath in, count 3.
- Breath out, count 4. And so on.
- As any thoughts come up and you lose count, start your count over again.
- When the timer goes off, your meditation is complete.

Visit the Wellness Library to engage with this practice via video and audio:
https://well4edu.org/w4e/zen-meditation

In the next chapter on mindfulness, we'll explore another meditation called mindfulness meditation in addition to other practices. Let's jump in!

Meditation   **159**

ADDITIONAL RESOURCES

If you'd like to learn more about the practice of meditation, I've included some resources. There are plenty more resources; these are the ones I personally recommend to others and go back to as references. Note that many more meditation-related book suggestions are in the next chapter, which is focused on mindfulness.

Books

Dr. Kristen Neff
- *Fierce Self-Compassion: How Women Can Harness Kindness to Speak Up, Claim Their Power, and Thrive*
- *Self-Compassion: The Proven Power of Being Kind to Yourself*

Sharon Salzberg
- *Insight Meditation*
- *Loving-Kindness: The Revolutionary Art of Happiness*
- *Real Happiness: The Power of Meditation – A 28-day Program*

Websites and Apps

Tara Brach – https://www.tarabrach.com/
Dr. Kristen Neff – https://self-compassion.org/
Sharon Salzberg – https://www.sharonsalzberg.com/

CHAPTER 8

Mindfulness

Originating from Hindu and Buddhist philosophies, mindfulness began over 2,500 years ago in the East. Jon Kabat-Zinn brought mindfulness to the West by founding the Center for Mindfulness at the University of Massachusetts Medical School. He also established the Oasis Institute for Mindfulness-Based Professional Education and Training. His technique, known as the Mindfulness-Based Stress Reduction (MBSR) program, is an eight-week program that focuses on stress reduction. Kabat-Zinn had the honor of studying with Buddhist teacher Thich Nhat Hanh, among others. In addition to Kabat-Zinn, Jack Kornfield and Sharon Salzberg are two other well-known mindfulness practitioners.

Mindfulness is the practice of bringing your attention or awareness to a point of focus or the present moment. Kabat-Zinn defines *mindfulness* as "awareness that emerges through paying attention on purpose, in the present moment, and non-judgmentally to the unfolding of experience moment by moment" (2003).

KEY CONCEPTS

There are Four Foundations of Mindfulness that stem from the Buddha (Gunaratana, 2012), including Mindfulness of the Body, Mindfulness of Feelings, Mindfulness of Mind, and Mindfulness of Dhamma. In addition to the Four Foundations, there are nine attitudes of mindfulness: nonjudging, patience, beginner's mind, trust, nonstriving, acceptance, letting go, gratitude, and generosity.

The Four Foundations of Mindfulness

The Four Foundations of Mindfulness include Mindfulness of the Body, Mindfulness of Feelings, Mindfulness of Mind, and Mindfulness of Dhamma.

1. **Mindfulness of the Body** – This includes mindfulness of the body's functioning, including breathing, flow of blood through the veins, digestion of food, as well as other internal bodily functioning. It also means our engagement in movement, including walking, sitting, standing, and other physical activities. It pertains to our awareness of the various parts of our bodies and an awareness of what is good for the body and what is not so good for the body.

2. **Mindfulness of Feelings** – This includes labeling of the feelings as pleasant, unpleasant, or neutral, a sense of whether our feelings are coming forward or going away, and an understanding of our feelings as internal to self or external to all beings.

3. **Mindfulness of Mind** – This includes identifying the qualities that exist in our mind and understanding the context of those qualities. For instance, is our habit of mind focused or unfocused? Is how we're looking at a situation expansive or limiting? Is what we're thinking tied to reality, or is it unrealistic? Do we need more time to develop our perspective, or is the idea we're having fully evolved?

4. **Mindfulness of Dhamma** – What does Dhamma mean? *Dhamma* translates to "our path or truth." Dhamma comprises several other concepts, including the Five Mental Hindrances, Five Aggregates of Clinging, Six Internal and External Senses, Seven Factors of Enlightenment, Four Noble Truths, and Noble Eightfold Path.

    (a) Five Mental Hindrances – The hindrances are anything that can cause us distractions.

       i. sense desire – desire-seeking through the five senses

       ii. ill will – feeling resentful, hostile, and bitter

       iii. sloth and torpor – not fully invested, unfocused

       iv. restlessness – inability to relax and concentrate

       v. worry and skeptical doubt – unable to trust in yourself and your abilities

(b) Five Aggregates of Clinging – The aggregates of clinging are both the physical and mental things we cling to in our lives.

   i. material form – the physical body

   ii. feelings – the physical sensations felt in the body

   iii. perceptions – observation and interpretation of experience

   iv. mental formations – thoughts and ideas

   v. consciousness – awareness of physical body, sensations, perceptions, and thoughts

(c) Six Internal and External Senses – The Six Internal and External Senses are the basis for our reality.

   i. eye and form – what we see

   ii. ear and sound – what we hear

   iii. nose and odor – what we smell

   iv. tongue and flavor – what we taste

   v. body and touch – what we feel

   vi. mind and mental objects – what we think

(d) Seven Factors of Enlightenment – The Seven Factors of Enlightenment or awareness are used to understand the path and describe enlightenment itself.

   i. mindfulness – awareness of our reality

   ii. investigation of Dhamma – discernment of reality

   iii. energy – effort

   iv. joy – contentment

   v. tranquility – relaxed state both in mind and body

   vi. concentration – one-pointed focus

   vii. equanimity – acceptance of what is

(e) Four Noble Truths – The Four Noble Truths explain our existence in life as suffering and provide ways to avoid suffering by releasing our propensity to cling and attach.

   i. suffering – the idea that there is always suffering in our lives, even when things are good

   ii. origin of suffering – the idea that our suffering stems from ego, and our cravings and ignorance

   iii. cessation of suffering – the idea that our suffering and our perspective of it is always changing as we continue to shift our mind's focus

   iv. path that leads to the cessation of suffering – the idea that meditation and our self-study toward wisdom can lead to freedom of suffering

(f) Noble Eightfold Path – The Noble Eightfold Path provides a guide to nonsuffering using eight precepts, which are divided into three parts:

   i. Ethical Conduct

   1. right speech – be kind in how you speak

   2. right action – be kind in how you behave

   3. right livelihood – be kind in the work you do

   ii. Mental Discipline

   1. right effort – be mindful of cultivating wholesome state of mind

   2. right mindfulness – be mindful of body, mind, feelings, and thoughts

   3. right concentration – be mindful of focusing on meaningful things

   iii. Wisdom

   1. right thought – extend love and nonviolence to all beings

   2. right understanding – accepting things as they are

Nine Attitudes of Mindfulness

The Nine Attitudes of Mindfulness are: nonjudging, patience, beginner's mind, trust, nonstriving, acceptance, letting go, gratitude, and generosity.

1. **Nonjudging** – Similar to the silent observer or witness in yogic practice, the mindful attitude of nonjudging asks us to objectively observe ourselves and our experiences without negative self-talk or judgment of others.

2. **Patience** – The age-old saying is "Patience is a virtue," and that it is. The mindful attitude of patience is about understanding that everything happens in its own time and accepting that the process can't be controlled or hurried.

3. **Beginner's Mind** – Seeing things with a fresh perspective, as if you're seeing them for the first time, with an openness to learning is the essence of the mindful attitude of a beginner's mind.

4. **Trust** – Having trust in yourself, your intuition, and in your experiences is the foundation of the mindful attitude of trust.

5. **Nonstriving** – Striving takes us out of ourselves and out of the present moment; the mindful attitude of nonstriving reminds us that we already are without doing.

6. **Acceptance** – A dose of reality, accepting things as they are, is the mindful attitude of acceptance.

7. **Letting Go** – The practice of nonattachment, the mindful attitude of letting go, allows us to release what we cling to, of what we hold on to.

8. **Gratitude** – By being grateful for who we are, the relationships we have with others, and the relationship we have with everything around us, we grow the source of joy in the present moment.

9. **Generosity** – Giving becomes a gift not only to others, but toward yourself, especially when you expect nothing in return.

PRACTICES

Now that you've learned a bit about mindfulness, it's time to practice. Before we jump in, let's revisit some key points from the "Preparation for the Practices" section of Chapter 4 so that we can be intentional about the mind-body connection as we practice mindfulness. This intentionality can help us reap all the benefits that result from the integration of the mind and the body.

As you engage in each mindfulness practice, ask yourself the following:

- What do I notice (in my body and/or mind)? (observe without judgment)
- What do I need in this moment? (observe without judgment and give yourself what you need to feel supported)

Revisit Deb Dana's four Rs:

1. **Recognize the autonomic state.** (How is my nervous system doing? Am I in flight/fight/freeze/fawn?)
2. **Respect the adaptive survival response.** (How am I reacting? Am I crying, shaking, feeling anxious? Whatever it is, I respect the response, as it is what my nervous system needs. I am not judging it.)
3. **Regulate or co-regulate into a ventral vagal state.** (What does my body and mind need now to feel safe? Do I need to hug myself? Do I need to lie down with my head on a pillow? Do I need a blanket to cover myself?)
4. **Re-story** (How can I re-frame my experience to see the learning that came up for me? What am I telling myself?)

Use the three perceptions to check in and stay grounded in the present moment:

- **Exteroception** – how we perceive external information from our senses – sight, sound, smell, taste, and touch.
  - What are five things that I can see?
  - What are four things that I can hear?
  - What are three things that I can smell?

- What are two things that I can taste?
- What is one thing that I can touch?
- **Interoception** – how we perceive sensations from inside the body, such as how we are able to feel our heartbeat and the air as it's moving into and out of our nose.
  - How does the air feel as I breathe in through my nose and out through my nose/mouth?
  - How does my heartbeat change as I engage in this practice?
- **Proprioception** – how we perceive our body in space by way of our movement and action.
  - How is my body situated in space?
  - How does my body interact with what's around me?

As with any practice, if you're new to it, please check with your doctor to make sure this activity is conducive to your wellbeing. Also, prior to practicing, please note any modifications and contraindications that are listed with each practice.

Vipassana Meditation

One of the oldest Buddhist meditation practices, Vipassana was founded in India 2,500 years ago. *Vipassana* is a Pali word that translates to "special seeing or clear-seeing". As Bhante Henepola Gunaratana (n.d.) shares, "Vipassana can be translated as *Insight*, a clear awareness of exactly what is happening as it happens." The practice is a way for us to focus on the body and the sensations within it. Concentrating on the breath, we become a silent observer during Vipassana practice.

FILL YOUR CUP

Vipassana meditation has the potential to cultivate calm, connection, focus, and intention.

Instructions:

- Decide on the amount of time you'd like to meditate.
- Find a quiet place that doesn't have distractions.
- Sit on the floor or in a chair with your feet on the ground.
- Straighten your back while relaxing the body.
- Close your eyes.
- Breathe naturally.
- Focus on the body's sensations, especially the breath in and breath out.
- Act as a silent, objective observer of your thoughts, feelings, and sensations.
- Refrain from judging yourself.
- As distractions come up, observe them and return to your breath.
- When time is up, finish your practice by taking a deep breath in and out through the nose.
- Gently open your eyes when you're ready.

Visit the Wellness Library to engage with this practice via video and audio:
  https://well4edu.org/w4e/vipassana-meditation

Body Scan

Body scans in the Buddhist tradition are done to simply observe the body. As you engage in the body scan, don't try to change anything or judge your experience. Even as thoughts arise, as is the case in the Vipassana meditation, observe those thoughts and come back to the body scan.

FILL YOUR CUP

Body scan has the potential to cultivate balance, calm, compassion, connection, forgiveness, grounding, heart-centeredness, patience, presence, and restoration.

Instructions:

- Find a quiet and comfortable place where you can sit or lie down. (Note: If you choose to lie down, try to remain awake.)
- If it feels okay for you to do so, close your eyes or have a gentle gaze.
- Keep the spine straight while the rest of your body is relaxed.
- Breathe in deeply, and as you exhale, relax the body.
- Allow the shoulders to loosen.
- Unclench the jaw.
- Soften your abdomen.
- Bring your awareness to the top of the head and notice anything that comes up for you.
- Drop down to your forehead, scrunch up the face and then relax it. Notice anything that comes up for you.
- Travel farther down to the eyes and cheekbones, to the nose and upper lip. Notice anything that comes up for you there. Perhaps you feel the air coming into and out of the nose as you breathe in and out.
- Drop to the mouth, the jaw, lips, tongue. Notice what's happening in the mouth. Is it dry or moist, is there tension? Noticing and acknowledging what is present.
- From the mouth, traveling to the neck and throat. Noticing the movement of the air as it travels in this part of your body. Noticing any physical experience without judgment.

- Moving to the shoulders and shoulder blades. Feeling the breath coming into that part of the body as you breathe in and out.
- Dropping into the arms and elbows and forearms. Noticing any sensations.
- Traveling down to your wrists and fingers. Perhaps noticing how they rest on your legs or in your lap.
- From the fingers moving back up the arms into the chest and noticing the rise and fall of your abdomen and chest as your breath comes into and out of the body.
- From the abdomen, moving down to the hips and the pelvis. Noticing any sensations without judgment as they arise.
- Dropping into the legs, into the thighs and knees and calves and shins. Feeling your clothing as they rest on these areas of the body.
- Traveling to the feet, starting at the ankle and moving from the heel to the arch of your foot and then to the ball of the foot and the toes. Perhaps you have tingling sensations in your toes. Just noticing without judgment whatever is coming up for you now.
- Visualizing the whole body from the crown of your head to the bottom of your feet as you practice this scan of the body, noticing and sensing the body now.
- As you are ready, gently open the eyes to reorient yourself in your space.

Visit the Wellness Library to engage with this practice via video and audio:

https://well4edu.org/w4e/body-scan

Gratitude List

Figure 8.1 Gratitude list.

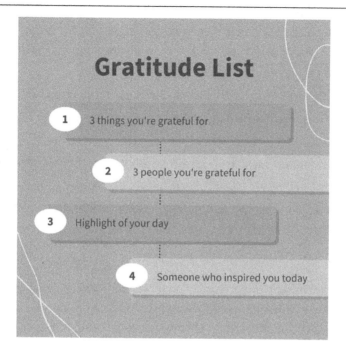

Starting a daily gratitude journal or a weekly gratitude list can help you reflect on things you're grateful for. It helps you keep a thankful perspective on the things that can easily be taken for granted in our lives. In just 15 minutes a day or a week, our gratitude practice can improve our mental health by boosting our mood and easing symptoms of anxiety and depression (Cregg and Cheavens 2021; Watkins et al. 2003).

FILL YOUR CUP

Keeping a gratitude list has the potential to cultivate connection, expansion, grounding, heart-centeredness, and presence.

Instructions:

- Choose a quiet and comfortable place where you like to reflect.
- Dedicate a notebook or a sketchpad and a special pen to your gratitude practice. Or you can use sticky notes so that you can post them as reminders in your space.
- On a daily or weekly basis, write 3–5 things you are grateful for.
- As you think of things that you're grateful for, be specific, focusing on experiences and people rather than physical possessions.
- If inspired to do so, share your list with a person you've mentioned so they know how you feel about them.
- At the end of the year, compile all your notes to reflect on a year of gratitude practice.

Tracking

To feel more present and grounded, you can try tracking. Tracking is especially helpful when our nerves are a bit frazzled, and our mind is distracted. It's a process of noticing what is around you, which can help bring you into the present moment.

FILL YOUR CUP

Tracking has the potential to cultivate balance, calm, connection, courage, grounding, presence, and restoration.

Instructions:

- Find a comfortable seated position.
- Take several breaths in and out, making the exhale just a bit longer than the inhale.
- Continue this breathing pattern.

- When you feel comfortable doing so, take your time as you look around your surroundings.
- Allow your eyes to settle on objects within your space.
- As your eyes settle on an object, say the name of the object aloud.
- If there is an object that feels more comforting to you, feel free to stay with that object and repeat the name of it aloud multiple times.
- Repeat this process until you feel grounded and calm.

Visit the Wellness Library to engage with this practice via video and audio:

https://well4edu.org/w4e/tracking

I hope you've enjoyed practicing some mindfulness activities. There are many others you can explore. We're going to move onto the practice of Qigong.

ADDITIONAL RESOURCES

If you'd like to learn more about the practice of mindfulness, I've included some resources. There are plenty more resources; these are the ones I personally recommend to others and go back to as references.

Books

Tara Brach
- *Radical Acceptance: Awakening the Love that Heals Fear and Shame*
- *Radical Acceptance: Embracing Your Life with the Heart of a Buddha*
- *Radical Compassion: Learning to Love Yourself and Your World with the Practice of RAIN*
- *True Refuge: Finding Peace and Freedom in Your Own Awakened*

Pema Chödrön
- *Awakening Loving-Kindness*
- *Comfortable with Uncertainty: 108 Teaching on Cultivating Fearlessness and Compassion*
- *Living Beautifully with Uncertainty and Change*
- *Start Where You Are: A Guide to Compassionate Living*
- *The Places that Scare You: A Guide to Fearlessness in Difficult Times*
- *When Things Fall Apart: Heart Advice for Difficult Times*

Jack Kornfield
- *A Lamp in the Darkness: Illuminating the Path Through Difficult Times*
- *No Time Like the Present: Finding Freedom and Joy Right Where You Are*

Thich Nhat Hanh
- *The Miracle of Mindfulness: An Introduction to the Practice of Meditation*
- *Peace is Every Step: The Path of Mindfulness in Everyday Life*

Sharon Salzberg
- *Real Change: Mindfulness to Heal Ourselves and the World*
- *Real Love: The Art of Mindful Connection*

Dr. Jon Kabat-Zinn
- *Meditation Is Not What You Think: Mindfulness and Why It Is So Important*

- *Mindfulness for Beginners*
- *Wherever You Go, There You Are: Mindfulness Meditation in Everyday Life*

Websites and Apps

Calm – https://www.calm.com
Headspace – https://www.headspace.com
Plum Village Zen Guided Meditation – https://plumvillage.app/
UCLA Mindful – UCLA Mindful via Apple Apps Store

CHAPTER 9

Qigong

The practices associated with Qigong originated in China over 5,000 years ago in the Daoist (Taoist) tradition. The literal translation consists of *Qi* (pronounced "chee"), meaning "energy," and *gong*, meaning "work or skill"; thus, the practice of Qigong is the practice of working with energy. *Qi* is often translated to "breath," "air," and "life force." There are key concepts of Qigong, and, depending on the strand of Qigong you practice, those key concepts can include breath, posture, movement, relaxation, and concentration/visualization.

In her book *Stone Medicine*, Leslie J. Franks (2016), a student of Dr. Jeffrey Yuen, an 88th-generation Daoist priest, talks about Qi using electricity as a metaphor:

> Its [electricity's] current moves through the utility company's electrical grid as pure energy. In our homes, though, we turn on a switch and the lamp illuminates the room, or we put a plug in the outlet and the digital face of a clock radio lights up... Qi has a similar flexibility of function... Qi suggests function, not substance. It is the reason blood and fluids circulate, but it is not the substances of blood and fluids themselves. It is the reason we as human beings are able to engage in relationship, but it is not the human being. (pp. 15–16)

It's important to note that there are many facets of Qigong, including healing geomancy and martial arts, to name a couple. This chapter concentrates on the healing nature of Qigong by way of breath, movement, and meditation.

KEY CONCEPTS

While there are many key concepts in Qigong, in this chapter, we're going to briefly explore the concepts of the three treasures, yin and yang, and the five elements.

Three Treasures

In Taoist philosophy, there are three treasures: Jing, Qi, and Shen.

- Jing – Jing is often referred to as *essence*. Jing is our physical body and the elements of that body, including what we have inherited genetically from our family. Through the practice of Qigong, "we begin to refine and strengthen our bodies by opening physical blockages and allowing the Qi and Blood to move more freely" (Franks 2016, p. 18). According to Kaptchuk:

  > Essence . . . is the texture that is specific to organic life. It is the stuff that makes living beings unique and distinct from inorganic things... In the usual Chinese manner that defies simple categories, it [Jing / Essence] is the potential, guidance, and actuality that shapes birth, development, maturation, decline, and death. (2000, p. 55)

- Shen – *Shen* is translated as "spirit." Spirit, according to Kaptchuk, is "more than mind-consciousness. Spirit is self-awareness that fosters the human experience of authenticity and personal meaning. Spirit allows self-reflection, art, morality, purpose, and values. It depends on self-relationship. . . Spirit is the process of self-examination, not its outcome" (2000, pp. 58–59). Shen is our connection to the transcendental. It arises from Jing; without Shen, there is no life. Kaptchuk also adds, "Spirit is felt whenever human consciousness forges compelling bonds and special relationships. Spirit is invoked by imagination, will, intention, awe, enchantment, and wonder" (2000, p. 58).

- Qi – We talked a little about Qi in its relation to Qigong already, but share a bit more about it here since it is key to the practice of Qigong. Qi, according to Kaptchuk, has to do with strength, effort, and capacity for work" (2000, p. 47). In addition to the physical aspect, psychologically, "Qi concerns desire, awareness of possibilities, considerations of options, resolution, and motivation" (Kaptchuk 2000, p. 47). Some of Qi's many functions, types, and disharmonies include the following.

- Functions of Qi:
  - Qi is the source of all movement and accompanies all movement.
  - Qi protects the body.
  - Qi is the source of collective and integrative change.
  - Qi ensures stability and governs retention.
  - Qi warms the body.
- Types of Qi:
  - Organ Qi (*zang-fu-zhi-qi*) – Each one of our organs has its own Qi.
  - Meridian Qi (*jing-luo-zhi-qi*) – Meridians are channels through which Qi travels throughout the body. We talk more about meridians in Chapter 10, which is focused on yin yoga.
  - Nutritive Qi (*ying-qi*) – Qi that resides in the blood and travels via the blood vessels.
  - Protective Qi (*wei-qi*) – Associated with fighting off external threats, Protective Qi is in the abdomen area and controls the "sweat glands and pores and moistens and protects the skin and hair."
  - Qi of the Chest or Ancestral Qi (*zong-qi*) – This Qi controls respiration and circulation in the chest.
- Disharmonies of Qi:
  - Deficient Qi (*qi-xu*) – This signifies a lack of the amount of Qi needed for vitality. Also includes Collapsed Qi (*qi-xian*).
  - Stagnant Qi (*qi-zhi*) – This condition is when the Qi gets stuck and doesn't flow as it should throughout the body.
  - Rebellious Qi (*qi ni*) – This is when the Qi is moving in the wrong direction. (Kaptchuk 2000, pp. 47–52)

The descriptions I've just shared are not exhaustive. There are many more texts that help to explain the Three Treasures, and you can find some of those listed at the end of this chapter in the "Additional Resources" section. From here, we're going to move on to talk about another major concept in Qigong called yin-yang theory.

Yin-Yang Theory

One of the more well-known aspects of Chinese medicine theory is that of yin-yang. Yin and yang are considered opposites while serving as two parts to a whole. You cannot have one without the other. Just like the mind and the body cannot be split, yin and yang cannot be separated (Dechar 2006). Dechar explains how an imbalance of yin or yang can cause issues in our mind and body:

> An excess accumulates on one side [yin or yang], bringing deficiency and exhaustion on the other. When yin and yang separate, we head away from movement toward impasse, away from life toward death. Unless there is a mingling of yin and yang, life processes are arrested and there can be no transformation. (2006, p. 18)

Yin and yang are like the chandra (moon) and surya (sun) channels in yogic philosophy. Yin and yang have varying qualities and are associated with different organs in the body.

- Yin:
  - "Yin grounds us into our bodies" (Franks 2016, p. 25).
  - "In Chinese philosophy, [yin is] the passive, negative, feminine polarity. In Chinese medicine, Yin means deficient. The Yin (internal) organs are the heart, lungs, liver, kidneys, spleen, and pericardium" (Yang 1989, p. 303).
  - Yin is cooling, calming, and restful.
  - Yin has form.
- Yang:
  - "In Chinese philosophy, [Yang is] the active positive, masculine polarity. In Chinese medicine, Yang means excessive, overactive, overheated. The Yang (or outer) organs are the gallbladder, small intestine, large intestine, stomach, bladder, and triple burner (Yang 1989, p. 302).
  - Yang is heating, energizing, and active.
  - Yang is formless.

In Qigong, movements, meditations, and breathwork can be structured to bring balance to yin and yang, depending on where the disharmony is in the body and mind. In the "Practices" section of this chapter, there will be some yin- and yang-focused techniques to support repletion, depending on which polarity is feeling blocked or deficient. The last key concept we cover before jumping into the practices is the five elements.

Five Elements

The five elements are: water, wood, fire, earth, and metal. Each one is associated with an organ, climate, season, emotion, and life cycle (among other aspects of life) as is shown in the following table.

Table 9.1 Five elements and their corresponding organ, climate, and season.

Element	Organ	Climate	Season	Emotion	Life Cycle
water	kidney	cold	winter	fear	gestation
wood	liver	windy	spring	anger	birth
fire	heart	heat	summer	joy	growth
earth	spleen	dampness	late summer	sympathy	transformation
metal	lung	dryness	autumn	grief	death

Based on the interactions of the five elements, each element influences the other. These interactions are illustrated in the following image.

Figure 9.1 Five elements.

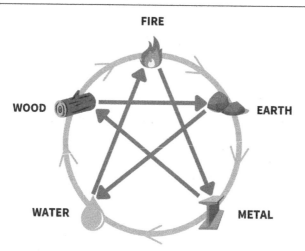

The arrows on the outer circle that are traveling clockwise show the creation cycle, while the arrows in the center of the circle illustrate the destruction cycle. Like the yin-yang theory, the five elements interact with each other via the creation and destruction cycles. As one waxes, the other wanes. When there are disruptions to these cycles, issues arise in the mind and/or body. For the creation cycle, which is illustrated by the arrows on the outer circle that are traveling clockwise, the following is the progression:

- Fire creates earth (joy nourishes sympathy)
- Earth creates metal (sympathy generates grief)
- Metal creates water (grief transforms to fear)
- Water creates wood (fear shifts to anger)
- Wood creates fire (anger liberates joy)

The destruction cycle, which is illustrated by the arrows in the center of the circle, demonstrates the following interactions:

- Water puts out fire (fear puts out excessive joy)
- Fire melts metal (joy melts grief)
- Metal splits wood (grief breaks up anger)
- Wood breaks up earth (anger dissolves overabundance of sympathy)
- Earth soaks up water (sympathy absorbs fear)

Like working with yin-yang to design an approach to your practice, you can do the same using the five elements. You can do this based on external seasons, for instance. Each of the five elements is aligned with a particular season. One core way of incorporating the five elements into your practice is by balancing and harmonizing your internal energies with those of the external season.

Another concept that is critical to Qigong practice is that of the meridians, pathways through which your energy flows throughout your body. The next chapter discusses more about the meridians.

A reminder that I am only covering the very surface of each of these key concepts that inform the practice of Qigong. If you're interested in learning more, there are additional resources that are listed in the "Additional Resources" section at the end of this chapter.

PRACTICES

Now that you've learned a bit about Qigong, it's time to practice. Before we jump in, let's revisit some key points from the "Preparation for the Practices" section of Chapter 4 so that we can be intentional about the mind-body connection as we practice Qigong. This intentionality can help us reap all the benefits that result from the integration of the mind and the body.

As you engage in each posture, ask yourself the following:

- What do I notice (in my body and/or mind)? (observe without judgment)
- What do I need in this moment? (observe without judgment and give yourself what you need to feel supported)

Revisit Deb Dana's four Rs:

1. **Recognize the autonomic state.** (How is my nervous system doing? Am I in flight/fight/freeze/fawn?)
2. **Respect the adaptive survival response.** (How am I reacting? Am I crying, shaking, feeling anxious? Whatever it is, I respect the response, as it is what my nervous system needs. I am not judging it.)
3. **Regulate or co-regulate into a ventral vagal state.** (What does my body and mind need now to feel safe? Do I need to hug myself? Do I need to lie down with my head on a pillow? Do I need a blanket to cover myself?)
4. **Re-story** (How can I reframe my experience to see the learning that came up for me? What am I telling myself?)

Use the three perceptions to check in and stay grounded in the present moment:

- **Exteroception** – how we perceive external information from our senses – sight, sound, smell, taste, and touch.
  - What are five things that I can see?
  - What are four things that I can hear?
  - What are three things that I can smell?
  - What are two things that I can taste?
  - What is one thing that I can touch?
- **Interoception** – how we perceive sensations from inside the body, such as how we are able to feel our heartbeat and the air as it's moving into and out of our nose.
  - How does the air feel as I breathe in through my nose and out through my nose/mouth?
  - How does my heartbeat change as I engage in this practice?
- **Proprioception** – how we perceive our body in space by way of our movement and action.
  - How is my body situated in space?
  - How does my body interact with what's around me?

As with any practice, if you're new to it, please check with your doctor to make sure this activity is conducive to your wellbeing. Also, prior to practicing, please note any modifications and contraindications that are listed with each practice.

Qigong Shaking

FILL YOUR CUP

Qigong Shaking helps to relieve the body and mind from anxiety, cultivating balance, calm, energy, grounding, openness, restoration, and vitality.

Contraindications: If you have neck issues, skip neck and head shaking and focus on your arms and legs.

Instructions:

- Stand with your feet flat on the floor and shoulder-width distance apart.
- Ensure your back is straight.
- Lightly flatten the curve of the lower (lumbar) back so that the abdomen and chest aren't arching forward.
- Allow your arms to rest at your sides.
- Begin to lightly shake your body starting at the wrists and arms.
- Allow the body to reverberate from the movements happening in your wrists and arms.
- Continue shaking the wrists and arms as you start to step side to side and shake the legs.
- If it's comfortable, feel free to gently bounce on the balls of your feet.
- Listen to your body to understand where the energy needs to be released from as you continue to gently shake from your head to your toes.
- Be mindful about the parts of your body you are protecting and make sure to continue to protect them as you need to, choosing to refrain from shaking the part that is not well or refraining from shaking altogether.

Modifications: Instead of shaking, slow movements in the body can serve as a gentle alternative.

Visit the Wellness Library to engage with this practice via video and audio:
https://well4edu.org/w4e/qigong-shaking

Sinking Qi Standing Meditation

FILL YOUR CUP

Sinking Qi Standing Meditation has the potential to cultivate balance, calm, energy, grounding, openness, presence, restoration, stability, and vitality.

Instructions:

- Stand comfortably with feet shoulder-width apart.
- Relax your shoulders down your back.
- Check your alignment: chin is down slightly so that the back of the neck is long; head comfortably back over the spine and not forward; shoulders should line up with the pelvis and the feet.
- Knees are soft and supportive, not locked.
- Lower (lumbar) spine is flat and not arched (which would thrust the abdomen forward and out of alignment). Picture a weight hanging suspended from the tailbone, and let the lumbar spine relax with the imagined weight.

- Arms hang at the sides of the body; you can also turn the hands so that the thumb and forefinger rest against your outer legs, making the back of the knuckles point forward and opening a little space in the armpits.

- As you relax into this stance, picture yourself as buoyant, as if there's a little space between all your joints and the top of your head is lifted slightly up toward the sky, elongating your spine.

- Eyes can be open, closed, or half-open (if open, the gaze is soft and focused on a point on the floor 10–15 feet in front of you).

- Begin to breathe into the abdomen, allowing the diaphragm to expand with each inhale and naturally return on the exhale.

- You can simply keep breathing like this if it's comfortable, or you can use the mind to focus on your feet. Feel how they connect to the floor or the ground beneath you. Feel the toes engage, yet relaxed; feel how the sides of your feet connect to the ground. See if you can sense how even the tops of your feet are rooted and connected.

- Continue to breathe and hold the stance if comfortable, allowing thoughts to rise in your mind without attaching to them. Return your mind to your feet and your connection to the ground if your attention wanders.

Modifications: The meditation, breathing, and visualizations can also be performed from a seated position: ensure that your back is comfortably straight and that your feet have good contact with the floor or ground. Knees should be at a comfortable 90-degree angle.

Visit the Wellness Library to engage with this practice via video and audio:

https://well4edu.org/w4e/standing-meditation-sinking-qi

Lift Hands – Harmonizing Qi

FILL YOUR CUP

Lift Hands – Harmonizing Qi practice has the potential to cultivate calm, connection, energy, expansion, heart-centeredness, openness, release, restoration, surrender, and vitality.

Instructions:

- Begin with feet together and one hand resting inside the other, palms up, in front of the body.
- Draw a deep breath into the abdomen; as you exhale, step out to the left so that your feet are shoulder-width distance apart.
- Spread the hands apart, rotating the palms to face down.
- Relax the shoulders and let the arms hang in front of the body, the hands close together and in front of the pelvis, palms facing inward.
- Make sure that the lower (lumbar) spine isn't arched but straight (imagine having a small weight suspended from the tailbone, pulling the low back into alignment).
- As you inhale, lift the arms lightly (hinging from the shoulders) up to chest height, maintaining a straight line from the forearm down through the wrist and hands (but keeping elbows relaxed, not locked).
- When the hands are at chest height, spread them wide to each side as if you're holding a giant ball between the palms (keep elbows relaxed).
- As you exhale, draw the hands back together in front of the chest and then let the arms drift down in front of the body back to their starting point.
- Repeat the exercise as much as feels good, maintaining a soft and airy feeling in the arms and coordinating with the breath.
- Close the exercise by inhaling and sweeping the arms up and out from the sides of the body until the hands hover just above the head, palms down. Exhale and slowly draw both hands down and toward the Dan

Tian (the body's energy storehouse), located one and a half inches below the navel. Align the palms and place both hands, palms-inward, over the Dan Tian as you take one more deep breath into the abdomen.

- Step the left foot in toward the right to finish.

Modifications: Can be performed while seated in a chair, preferably with feet firmly on the ground

Visit the Wellness Library to engage with this practice via video and audio:

https://well4edu.org/w4e/lift-hands-harmonizing-qi

Balancing Yin and Yang Sitting Meditation

FILL YOUR CUP

Balancing Yin and Yang Sitting Meditation has the potential to cultivate balance, calm, energy, grounding, presence, restoration, and stability.

Instructions:

- Sit with your hands on your lap.
- Allow the palms to face down or face in toward your body.
- If you're sitting in a chair, keep your feet flat on the floor and your knees at a 90-degree angle.
- Keep your spine straight and relaxed.
- Relax your shoulders.
- Slightly flatten the curve of the lower (lumbar) back so that the abdomen and chest aren't arching forward.
- Lower your chin slightly so that the back of your neck is long and relaxed.

- Keep your head comfortably in line with your spine (do not thrust it forward).
- Keep your tongue gently on the roof of your mouth behind your teeth (or if you have high blood pressure, you can place your tongue behind the bottom teeth inside your mouth).
- Close your eyes if it's comfortable for you or keep a soft gaze.
- Breathe in slowly and deeply through the nose (if possible) and into the abdomen, letting the diaphragm expand as you inhale.
- As you continue to breathe deeply and gently, imagine that roots are growing down from your feet deep into the earth and out in all directions.
- As you breathe in, draw the restoring yin energy from the earth, up the legs, and into the body's energy storehouse – the Dan Tian – located an inch and a half below the navel and in the center of the body. As you exhale, the yin energy collects and gently condenses into the Dan Tian.
- Hold this visualization for a minute or two, or if comfortable, as you continue to breathe steadily and gently.
- Next, visualize the sun shining above you, shedding its warmth and light on the top of your head, neck, and shoulders and down the arms. This is warm yang energy, which travels down through the body into the Dan Tian as you inhale, collecting at the Dan Tian as you exhale.
- Hold this visualization for a minute or two, or if comfortable for you, as you continue to breathe steadily and gently.
- If you'd like, and if it's comfortable, you can try to hold both images at once to draw in the yin-yang energies. Or you can focus on the one you feel you need (you can also emphasize yang energy by keeping the palms facing up or yin by facing the palms down).
- Continue the meditation for as long as it is comfortable for you. If you begin to feel agitated or restless, or if you experience any pain or discomfort in your body from sitting, stop the meditation session. (Over time, longer sessions will become easier.)

Modifications: The meditation, breathing, and visualizations can also be performed standing or lying down.

Visit the Wellness Library to engage with this practice via video and audio:

https://well4edu.org/w4e/balancing-yin-and-yang

Five Element Qigong to Balance the Organs

FILL YOUR CUP

Five Element Qigong to Balance the Organs has the potential to cultivate balance, calm, connection, energy, expansion, heart-centeredness, openness, release, restoration, surrender, and vitality.

Instructions:

- **Wood Element**
  - Begin this practice by standing with your feet hips-width apart.
  - Starting with the wood element. Step the feet together, and as you inhale, step the feet apart to about shoulder-width distance bending the knees as you place the palms of the hands against the inner thighs right above the knees and guide your hands up toward your pelvis and up the sides of your abdomen to just below your rib cage, tracing the liver meridian. Straighten the legs as you bring your hands up.
  - On the exhale, pressing the heels of the hands in toward the abdomen and down through the pelvis as you massage the organs of the gallbladder and the liver, bending the knees as you come down through the pelvis. When the hands are at the base of the pelvis, breathe in and let your arms float gently up to shoulder height as you bring the feet together and straighten the legs to standing. Arms float down to the sides of your body as you exhale.
  - In this practice, you're working with the liver.

- Do this 5–10 more times, keeping the breath and movement slow and steady. As you do the movements, think about breathing in kindness (sign of balance in the wood element) and exhaling out anger and frustration (sign of imbalance in the wood element).

- Before moving onto the fire element, perform a clearing movement by stepping the feet hips-width distance apart or wider, bending the arms to 90 degrees, sweeping them out from the centerline of the body and up to a little higher than shoulder height and then bringing the hands toward the centerline of the body, palms facing down as you slowly lower them, releasing anything you need to on the way down. Finishing this clearing movement by allowing the hands, one over the other, to rest on the Dan Tian, located in the lower abdomen.

- **Fire Element**
  - Begin this practice by standing with your feet hips-width apart.
  - Step the feet together, and as you inhale, step the feet apart to a little more than shoulder-width distance bending the knees as you bring the inner edges of your pinkies together and bring the arms overhead as you straighten the legs.
  - Then bring the backs of the hands together and trace down through the centerline as you bend the knees into a squat.
  - Inhale the arms out to shoulder height away from the body as you straighten the legs and exhale the hands down to your sides.
  - Bring your feet together.
  - In this practice, you're working with the heart and small intestine.
  - Do this 5–10 more times, keeping the breath and movement slow and steady. As you do the movements, think about breathing in compassion and generosity (sign of balance in the fire element) and exhaling out anxiety and restlessness (sign of imbalance in the fire element).
  - Before moving onto the earth element, perform a clearing movement by stepping the feet hips-width distance apart or wider, bending the arms to 90 degrees sweeping them out from the centerline of the body and up to a little higher than shoulder height and then bringing the hands toward the centerline of the body, palms facing down as you

slowly lower them, releasing anything you need to on the way down. Finishing this clearing movement by allowing the hands, one over the other, to rest on the Dan Tian, located in the lower abdomen.

- **Earth Element**
  - Begin this practice by standing with your feet hips-width apart.
  - Step the feet together.
  - Step the left foot out, both arms swing out toward the left foot, palms facing up, then the right hand turns palm down as the left hand stays palm up and leads a deep twist over toward the right side of the body.
  - Then bend at the hips into a deep squat as you come back to center and the left arm sweeps down toward the earth and out. As you come up from the squat, and bring both arms, palms facing down, at shoulder height and gently lower them to your sides and bring feet together.
  - Step the right foot out, both arms swing out toward the right foot, palms facing up, then the left hand turns palm down as the right hand stays palm up and leads a deep twist over toward the left side of the body.
  - Bend at the hips into a deep squat as you come back to center and the right arm sweeps down toward the earth and out. As you come up from the squat, and bring both arms, palms facing down, at shoulder height and gently lower them to your sides and bring feet together.
  - In this practice, you're working with the spleen.
  - Do this 5–10 more times, keeping the breath and movement slow and steady. As you do the movements, think about breathing in steadiness, sincerity, and sympathy (sign of balance in the earth element) and exhaling out obsession and worry (sign of imbalance in the earth element).
  - Before moving onto the metal element, perform a clearing movement by stepping the feet hips-width distance apart or wider, bending the arms to 90 degrees, sweeping them out from the centerline of the body and up to a little higher than shoulder height and then bringing the hands toward the centerline of the body, palms facing down as you slowly lower them, releasing anything you need to on the way down.

Finishing this clearing movement by allowing the hands, one over the other, to rest on the Dan Tian, located in the lower abdomen.

- **Metal Element**
  - Begin this practice by standing with your feet hips-width apart.
  - Step the feet together.
  - As you inhale, step the feet apart to a little more than shoulder-width distance as you bring the inner edges of your hands parallel at the centerline of the body as you sweep them from below the abdomen to up above the head. Then exhale, bringing your hands to either side of your chest with palms facing away from the body (as if you're on the floor about to do a push-up), and as you push your hands out and away from the body, come into a deep squat. As you inhale, slowly come up from your deep squat while you keep your arms at shoulder height and flip the palms of the hands to face down, and exhale as you float the hands down to your sides.
  - In this practice, you're working with the lungs.
  - Do this 5–10 more times, keeping the breath and movement slow and steady. As you do the movements, think about breathing in refinement, slowing down, and letting go (sign of balance in the metal element) and exhaling out greed, sadness, and grief (sign of imbalance in the metal element).
  - Before moving onto the water element, perform a clearing movement by stepping the feet hips-width distance apart or wider, bending the arms to 90 degrees, sweeping them out from the centerline of the body and up to a little higher than shoulder height and then bringing the hands toward the centerline of the body, palms facing down as you slowly lower them, releasing anything you need to on the way down. Finishing this clearing movement by allowing the hands, one over the other, to rest on the Dan Tian, located in the lower abdomen.
- **Water Element**
  - Begin this practice by standing with your feet hips-width apart.

- Step the feet together.

- As you inhale, step the left foot out to a little more than shoulder-width and sweep the arms back and behind you with palms facing up while doing a slight backbend.

- Once the hands come overhead, the upper body follows the arms as you bend at the hips down into a forward bend, bending the knees as needed. Taking the fingers to the back of the legs and as you come up, tracing the fingers along the backs of the legs until you come to the hips. You are tracing the urinary bladder meridian. At the hips, make fists of your hands and lightly tap the kidneys with your fist (kidneys are located right above your belt line in the lower back). Exhale as you trace back down along the backs of your legs as you come back into your forward bend and bring the fingers to the inner legs, inhaling as you trace up toward the pelvis. Exhale the feet together.

- In this practice, you're working with the kidneys.

- Do this 5–10 more times, keeping the breath and movement slow and steady. As you do the movements, think about breathing in persever-ance, fluidity, steadiness, stamina, and energy (sign of balance in the water element) and exhaling out fear and trepidation (sign of imbal-ance in the water element).

- As we close the practice, perform a clearing movement by stepping the feet hips-width distance apart or wider, bending the arms to 90 degrees, sweeping them out from the centerline of the body and up to a little higher than shoulder height and then bringing the hands toward the centerline of the body, palms facing down as you slowly lower them, releasing anything you need to on the way down. Finish this clearing movement by allowing the hands, one over the other, to rest on the Dan Tian, located in the lower abdomen. Find a greater state of balance and harmony as we finish this practice, which brings balance to all the major organs of the body and their associated ele-ments of wood, fire, earth, metal, and water.

There are many other practices in Qigong that you can explore. Let's move onto the practice of yin yoga.

Visit the Wellness Library to engage with this practice via video
and audio:

> https://well4edu.org/w4e/five-element-wood
> https://well4edu.org/w4e/five-element-fire
> https://well4edu.org/w4e/five-element-earth
> https://well4edu.org/w4e/five-element-metal
> https://well4edu.org/w4e/five-element-water

ADDITIONAL RESOURCES

If you'd like to learn more about the practice of Qigong, I've included some resources below. There are plenty more resources; these are the ones I personally recommend to others and go back to as references.

Books

Lorie Eve Dechar – *Five Spirits: Alchemical Acupuncture for Psychological and Spiritual Healing*

Leslie J. Frank – *Stone Medicine: A Chinese Medical Guide to Healing with Gems and Minerals*

Dr. Ted Kaptchuk – *The Web That Has No Weaver: Understanding Chinese Medicine*

David Palmer – *Qigong Fever: Body, Science, and Utopia in China*

Elisa Rossi – *Shen: Psycho-Emotional Aspects of Chinese Medicine*

Dr. Yang, Jwing-Ming – *The Root of Chinese Qigong: Secrets for Health, Longevity, & Enlightenment*

Zhang Yu Huan & Ken Rose – *A Brief History of Qi*

Websites

Mimi Kuo-Deemer – https://www.mkdeemer.com/

Qi Gong Institute of Rochester – https://www.qigongrochester.com/

CHAPTER 10

Yin Yoga

This chapter is purposely situated after the Qigong chapter because much of the key concepts from Qigong are applicable to yin yoga, including the three treasures, yin-yang theory, and the five elements. As mentioned in Chapter 9, another key concept of Qigong that is also associated with yin yoga is the meridian system. We talk more about those as a key concept in this chapter.

So, you might be wondering why not just call the practice "yin" if the practice stems from Taoist philosophy? Why add "yoga"? This is because yin yoga also has connections to the yogic tradition. Specifically, yin yoga incorporates the chakras that are discussed in Chapter 5. Each chakra is aligned with a meridian that is from the Taoist philosophy. We share that in the "Key Concepts" section.

Before we jump into the key concepts, let's define yin yoga. Yin yoga is a meditative practice where you hold postures for an extended amount of time. The postures themselves are mostly done on the floor with props (pillows, bolsters, yoga blocks, yoga straps). Yin yoga does not focus on the muscles, which are targeted more in the yoga practice that is introduced and covered in Chapter 5; rather, in yin yoga postures, we focus on putting a gentle amount of stress and tension on the deep connective tissues of the body, including the joints, ligaments, tendons, cartilage, and fascia. Here's a quick anatomy lesson before we move on:

- Joints – where two or more bones meet
- Ligaments – connective tissue that connects one or more bones to other bones
- Tendons – connective tissue that connects bones to muscles
- Cartilage – tissue that supports the end of bones where they junction with joints

- Fascia – thin web of connective tissue that "surrounds and holds every organ, blood vessel, bone, nerve fiber, and muscle in place" (Johns Hopkins Medicine, n.d.)

    (a) Superficial fascia – fascia associated with the skin

    (b) Deep fascia – fascia associated with the blood vessels, bones, nerves, and muscles

    (c) Visceral fascia – fascia associated with the internal organs

The practice of yin yoga increases circulation and mental focus, balances the organs and releases fascia, and improves joint mobility and flexibility. The practice of yin yoga allows you to feel the body's sensations without being overwhelmed by them. Let's learn more about yin yoga's key concepts, including its three tattvas and the meridians.

KEY CONCEPTS

Three Tattvas

According to Sarah Powers, author of *Insight Yoga*, yin yoga is structured by three tattvas, or principals, that are critical to keeping you safe as you engage in this transformative practice. These tenets include: (1) come into the pose to an appropriate depth or "coming to your edge," (2) resolve to remain still or "practicing stillness for an extended time," and (3) hold the pose for time. I refer to these tattvas in this chapter as the following:

1. Come to your edge.
2. Practice stillness.
3. Hold for extended time.

Let's explore each of these a bit more.

Come to Your Edge   I think this tenet of the three is most important for your safety when practicing yin yoga. In yin yoga, as previously mentioned, we're putting a small amount of tension on the body's connective tissues. It is vitally important to not go beyond your edge in yin yoga, as that could result in injury. So how do you figure out what your edge is? I greatly appreciate the way my teacher – Sagel Urlacher – talked about this.

Sagel shared the Goldilocks method, which was also shared in Bernie Clark's *The Complete Guide to Yin Yoga: The Philosophy & Practice of Yin Yoga.*

Figure 10.1 The Goldilocks method.

So, what does the story of *Goldilocks and the Three Bears* have to do with the practice of yin yoga. This story aligns to the practice of *coming to your edge* in yin yoga. In each posture you practice, you want to avoid coming to a place that puts too much stress or tension on your body. You want to avoid coming to a place that puts too little stress or tension on your body. Instead, you want to come to a place that is "just right" for your body. If you were to put this "just right" on a scale of 1 to 10, where 1 is "too little" and 10 is "too much," you'll want to come to a 3 or 4 so that you're closer to the "too little" side rather than the "too much" side of the scale. You'll want to find the place where it's challenging but not uncomfortable or painful.

Keep in mind that if you're practicing yin yoga (or any form of yoga) with other people, you do not want to compare yourself to others. Why is that? Oftentimes, when we compare ourselves to those around us, we think that we should be doing what they are doing, and in that practice of comparison, we can inadvertently hurt ourselves by going beyond what is okay for our own bodies. Always listen to your own body and mind to keep yourself safe in your practice. As one of my mentors who also served on our board of directors, Dr. Wendy Drexler, said:

> "Practice" is a wonderful word because it gives the sense that we can continue to change and grow. The goal is not achieving but practicing the postures as a means to changing our bodies and minds over time. When I think about it as a practice, I'm less likely to compare my practice to anyone else. Just like practicing my guitar. There are some things I can do that others can't. There are many things I can't do that others can. I am on my own journey. (Personal correspondence July 7, 2022)

Practice Stillness The second tattva is practicing stillness, including stillness within the mind, stillness within the breath, and stillness within the body. Stillness within the mind is practiced by acknowledging anything that comes up without judgment and then coming back to the breath. Stillness within the breath is allowing the breath to be natural and relaxed while noticing how the posture might affect the breath and then coming back to natural breathing. Stillness within the body is finding a place where you don't feel like you have to move.

The exception to practicing stillness is when we feel like we need to move, for our bodies, our breath, or our minds. When would this be the case? As you practice yin yoga, even though you are not moving, the postures often continue to intensify for the body, the breath, and the mind. If your scale starts to creep up to a 5 or 6 as you hold the posture either for your body, your breath, or your mind, you can always back off to come to a 3 or 4 again. It is okay to back off. Similarly, you might find that as you stay in a posture, you're continuing to find ease and your 3 or 4 might go to a 1 or 2. If that's the case, you can choose to go a bit deeper to get back to a 3 or 4.

Hold for Extended Time   Postures in yin yoga are held for an extended amount of time in order to apply a healthy amount of stress on the connective tissues. Holding postures for an extended time is the third tattva. Why is it important to hold yin yoga postures for an extended amount of time? By holding yin yoga postures, your body's connective tissues have the opportunity to stress. According to Paul Grilley, author of *Yin Yoga: Principles & Practice*, connective tissues act differently than muscles because they take much longer to respond. In fact, Grilley shared, "Connective tissues resist brief stresses but slowly change when a moderate stress is maintained for three-to-five minutes" (2012, p. 21). When you hold the postures, make sure that your muscles are relaxed. Grilley explains why it's so important for our muscles to be relaxed during yin yoga practice:

> There are three layers to a joint: the bones, the connective tissue, and the muscles that move the bones. When the muscles are relaxed, the bones can be pulled apart and the connective tissue is stretched. When the muscles are tensed, the bones are pulled tightly together and the connective tissue is not stretched. (p. 24)

Because your connective tissues can be fragile after holding yin postures, you want to make sure to transition out of the posture very slowly and follow up the posture with a counter posture. While counter postures are separate practices themselves, they are shared as integral parts of each of the postures in the "Practices" section of this chapter.

Before we dive into experiencing some yin yoga postures, let's talk about the meridians and why they, in collaboration with chakras, are important to the practice of yin yoga.

Meridians

Meridians are pathways through which our Qi flows to and from our vital organs. Based on Taoist philosophy, a block or slowing down of the flow of Qi has the potential to cause disease in the body and mind. There are 12 organ meridians in the Taoist system that are associated with the practice of Qigong. The 12 organ meridians are the Lung, Large Intestine, Stomach, Spleen, Heart, Small Intestine, Urinary Bladder, Kidney, Gall Bladder, Liver, Pericardium, and Triple Heater. The Pericardium and Triple Heater are not included in the meridian descriptions in this chapter because they are not included as often as the other meridians in yin yoga poses.

Why is it so important to understand the meridians when we're practicing yin yoga? The meridians can alert us when we are in balance and out of balance based on the attributes we're exhibiting. These attributes can be positive or negative, and are aligned with the yogic tradition's chakra system. The information presented here is a brief overview of each of the meridians, including their location, their corresponding chakra, and indicators for when they are balanced and imbalanced.

The information shared about the meridians comes from a number of sources, including: Sagel Urlacher's *Yin Yoga & Meditation: A Mandala Map for Practice, Teaching, and Beyond*; Sarah Powers' *Insight Yoga: An Innovative Synthesis of Traditional Yoga, Meditation, and Eastern Approaches to Healing and Well-Being*; Dr. Hiroshi Motoyama's *Theories of the Chakras: Bridge to Higher Consciousness*; Biff Mithoefer's *The Yin Yoga Kit: The Practice of Quiet Power*; Paul Grilley's *Yin Yoga: Principles & Practice*; and Bernie Clark's *The Complete Guide to Yin Yoga: The Philosophy & Practice of Yin Yoga*. Note that 10 meridians are explained as interdependent pairs of one yin meridian and one yang meridian.

Liver and Gall Bladder Meridians The Liver (yin organ) meridian flows up from the big toe up through the inside of the thighs. Once it reaches the pelvis, it flows up through the right side of the body up through the right chest and neck, over the mouth and up to the right side of the head. The Gall Bladder (yang organ) meridian flows down on the right side of the head down the right side of the neck and down the right side of the body with an internal path through the liver and gallbladder. Finally, it flows down the outside of the knee and ends in the foot at the tip of the fourth toe.

The Liver meridian, specifically, "governs the overall healthy flow of energy" (Powers 2008, p. 58). The Gall Bladder meridian "relates to our ability to follow our path in life, to avoid deviating or being put off by external influences" (Powers 2008, p. 59). Of the five elements, the Liver and Gall Bladder meridians are associated with the wood element and correspond to our right to live (Powers 2008, p. 57).

The corresponding chakra for the Liver and Gall Bladder is the solar plexus chakra. When in balance, the Liver and Gall Bladder meridians can cultivate compassion, clear thinking, wisdom, self-esteem, and confidence. When imbalanced, the Liver and Gall Bladder meridians can result in anger and shame.

Heart and Small Intestine Meridians The Heart meridian flows out from the heart and down the arms to the end of the pinky fingers. Another channel runs through the diaphragm and small intestine. The third channel of the Heart meridian runs out from the heart and up to the throat and tongue and to its final destination – the eye. The Small Intestines meridian flow starts in the pinky finger and flows up via the outer arm to the shoulder. At that point, the Small Intestines meridian divides into two channels, one of which intersects the organs of the heart, diaphragm, stomach, and small intestine. The other channel flows up through the face to the corner of the eye and over to the ear.

The Heart and Small Intestine meridians oversee the Qi's responsibility to control the blood. In Chinese medicine, "blood is considered the yin aspect of chi . . . blood gives us the capacity to embrace and be comfortable with what has already been created" (Powers 2008, p. 87). Of the five elements, Heart and Small Intestine are associated with fire and correspond to our "right to love and be loved" (Mithoefer 2006, p. 28).

The corresponding chakra for the Heart and Small Intestine is the heart chakra. When in balance, the Heart and Small Intestine meridians can cultivate openness, love, connection, and a love of life. When imbalanced, the

Heart and Small Intestine meridians can result in hate, grief, a closed-off nature, and depression.

Spleen and Stomach Meridians   The Spleen (yin organ) meridian flows up the body starting from the inside of the big toes up through the inner legs and into the groin. From there, the Spleen meridian travels through the stomach and spleen and up through the diaphragm, heart, and neck, and stops at the base of the tongue. The Stomach (yang organ) meridian flows from the nose and down through the diaphragm, stomach, and spleen. From there, the Stomach meridian flows down the top of the leg and finishes its flow at the pointer toe.

The Spleen and Stomach meridians are about clarity of thinking and action from a sense of feeling at ease with being our authentic selves. Of the Five Elements, Spleen and Stomach meridians are associated with earth and correspond to our "right to act" (Mithoefer 2006, p. 28).

The corresponding chakra for the Spleen and Stomach meridians is the solar plexus chakra. When in balance, the Spleen and Stomach meridians can cultivate equanimity, balanced power, willpower, and autonomy. When imbalanced, the Spleen and Stomach meridians can result in anxiety and unwillingness to act.

Lung and Large Intestine Meridians   The Lung meridian starts off its flow in the center of the body coming up through the large intestine then moves through the diaphragm and lungs. From there, the Lung meridian flows through the clavicle to the inside of the arm and finishes at the tip of the thumb. The Large Intestine flows from the index finger and up through the back of the arm into the shoulder. It then breaks off into two channels, one of which travels into the neck and mouth to the side of the nose. The other channel travels down through the lungs, diaphragm, and large intestine.

These two meridians are critical to both sustaining life and letting go of anything that's no longer serving the body in both a physical and mental capacity. The lungs act to "replenish our energy" and "bolster[s] every cell in our body" (Powers 2008, pp. 85–86). Of the five elements, Lung and Large Intestines meridians are associated with metal and correspond to our "right to speak and be heard" (Mithoefer 2006, p. 28).

The corresponding chakra for the Lung and Large Intestines is the throat chakra. When in balance, the Lung and Large Intestine meridians can cultivate courage, communication, and creative self-expression. When imbalanced, the Lung and Large Intestines meridians can result in lying, sorrow, sadness, and miscommunication.

Kidney and Urinary Bladder Meridians The Kidney (yin organ) meridian flows up from the toes, up the inside of the thighs. Once it reaches the pelvis it flows up the internal body to the belly button and splits in two, flowing up the middle of the chest to the clavicle and stopping at the throat. The Urinary Bladder (yang organ) meridian flows down the back body. From the inner eye sockets, two parallel channels flow over the head and down to the neck where they each split. At the point of that split, two double parallel lines flow down to the sacrum area. The meridian then moves over the gluteus down to the backs of the knees, through the calves to the heels and then along the edge of the feet out to the pinky toes.

These two meridians are critical to keep balanced as the other vital organs depend on them to function. Specifically, the Kidney meridian "is responsible for a vibrant quality of inner energy" (Powers 2008, p. 58). According to Powers, these two meridians "are a storehouse of vital energy" (2008, p. 31). Of the five elements, Kidney and Urinary Bladder are associated with water and correspond to our "right to be" and "right to feel" (Mithoefer 2006, p. 28).

The corresponding chakras for the Kidney and Urinary Bladder are the root and sacral chakras. When in balance, the Kidney and Urinary Bladder meridians can cultivate grounding, safety, vitality, courage, and a sense of belonging and feeling. When imbalanced, the Kidney and Urinary Bladder meridians can result in fearfulness and guilt.

PRACTICES

Now that you've learned a bit about yin yoga, it's time to practice. Before we jump in, let's revisit some key points from the "Preparation for the Practices" section of Chapter 4 so that we can be intentional about the mind-body connection as we practice yin yoga. This intentionality can help us reap all the benefits that result from the integration of the mind and the body.

As you engage in each posture, ask yourself the following:

- What do I notice (in my body and/or mind)? (observe without judgment)
- What do I need in this moment? (observe without judgment and give yourself what you need to feel supported)

Revisit Deb Dana's four Rs:

1. **Recognize the autonomic state.** (How is my nervous system doing? Am I in flight/fight/freeze/fawn?)

2. **Respect the adaptive survival response.** (How am I reacting? Am I crying, shaking, feeling anxious? Whatever it is, I respect the response, as it is what my nervous system needs. I am not judging it.)

3. **Regulate or co-regulate into a ventral vagal state.** (What does my body and mind need now to feel safe? Do I need to hug myself? Do I need to lie down with my head on a pillow? Do I need a blanket to cover myself?)

4. **Re-story** (How can I reframe my experience to see the learning that came up for me? What am I telling myself?)

Use the three perceptions to check in and stay grounded in the present moment:

- **Exteroception** – how we perceive external information from our senses – sight, sound, smell, taste, and touch.
  - What are five things that I can see?
  - What are four things that I can hear?
  - What are three things that I can smell?
  - What are two things that I can taste?
  - What is one thing that I can touch?
- **Interoception** – how we perceive sensations from inside the body, such as how we are able to feel our heartbeat and the air as it's moving into and out of our nose.
  - How does the air feel as I breathe in through my nose and out through my nose/mouth?
  - How does my heartbeat change as I engage in this practice?
- **Proprioception** – how we perceive our body in space by way of our movement and action.
  - How is my body situated in space?
  - How does my body interact with what's around me?

As with any practice, if you're new to it, please check with your doctor to make sure this activity is conducive to your wellbeing. Also, prior to practicing, please note any modifications and contraindications that are listed with each practice.

Butterfly

Figure 10.2 Butterfly.

FILL YOUR CUP

Butterfly has the potential to cultivate letting go, openness, perspective, release, surrender, and trust.

Butterfly affects the Kidney and Liver meridians and the root and sacral chakras.

Contraindications: Sciatica

Instructions:

- From a seated position, bring the soles of your feet together.
- Slide the soles of your feet away from you.
- Allow your back to round.
- Fold forward from the hips, coming to your edge (a 3 or 4 out of 10).
- Lightly rest your hands on your feet or on the floor in front of you.
- Allow your head to hang down toward your heels.
- Hold posture for five minutes while breathing normally.
- After five minutes, slowly lift the head.
- To come out of the posture, use your hands on the outside of your knees to lift the legs up from butterfly position.
- Lean back onto the floor behind you by placing your hands about a foot or so away from your body.
- Allow the knees to act like windshield wipers going back and forth from side to side for about a minute.

Modifications: Elevate the hips with a bolster; if your neck is uncomfortable, support it with your hands, a block, or a bolster; you can practice doing half butterfly with the other leg straight out.

Visit the Wellness Library to engage with this practice via video and audio:
   https://well4edu.org/w4e/butterfly

Frog

Figure 10.3 Frog.

FILL YOUR CUP

Frog* has the potential to cultivate balance, connection, grounding, openness, presence, stability, strength, and trust.

Frog affects the Kidney, Urinary Bladder, Liver, and Spleen meridians and the root, sacral, and solar plexus chakras.

Contraindications: Back and knee injuries

Instructions:

(*Note there are two options to come into Frog, including from Child's Pose and from tabletop.)

- Start in Child's Pose.
  - Slide both hands forward.
  - Separate the knees but remain sitting on the heels. This is known as tadpole.
  - Separate the feet as wide as the knees.
  - Extend one arm out at a time.
- Begin in a tabletop position on your hands and knees.
  - Place hands underneath shoulders and knees below the hips.
  - Engage your core.
  - Slowly move your right knee out toward the side with the knee in line with the right heel.
  - Align left knee in line with the left heel.
  - Continue opening your hips as you turn your feet out toward the side.
  - Slowly lower your elbows and forearms with the palms flat on the floor or pressed together.
  - Press hips backward until you feel a deep stretch in the hips and inner thighs.
- Come to your edge (a 3 or 4 out of 10).
- Hold for five minutes.
- To come out of the posture, slowly move yourself forward using your hands and forearms.
- This action will also provide you an opportunity to straighten the legs.
- Once your legs are straightened out, bend the knees and windshield wiper the legs back and forth for a minute.

Modifications: You could do half frog instead of full; use a bolster under the body to give a bit of relief to the groin area.

Visit the Wellness Library to engage with this practice via video and audio:
https://well4edu.org/w4e/frog

Dragon

Figure 10.4 Dragon.

FILL YOUR CUP

Dragon has the potential to cultivate balance, focus, grounding, stability, and strength.

Dragon affects the Stomach, Spleen, Liver, Gall Bladder, and Kidney meridians and the root, sacral, and solar plexus chakras.

Contraindications: Be mindful if you have knee conditions.

Instructions:

- Begin on your hands and knees.
- Step one foot between your hands.
- Walk the front foot forward until the knee is right above the heel.
- Slide the back knee back as far as you can to get to your comfortable edge (a 3 or 4 out of 10).
- Keep hands on either side of the front foot.
- Hold for five minutes.
- Before moving to the other leg, slowly bring your front leg back to meet the back leg and come up into a Downward Dog and perhaps follow it up with a Child's Pose.

- Use the preceding instructions to do the other leg.
- When you're finished with the other leg, slowly bring your front leg back to meet the back leg and come up into a Downward Dog and perhaps follow it up with a Child's Pose.

Modifications: Support your knee that's on the floor with a blanket; use a block on either side of your foot to provide support to your hands and shoulders.

Visit the Wellness Library to engage with this practice via video and audio:
   https://well4edu.org/w4e/dragon

Caterpillar

Figure 10.5 Caterpillar.

FILL YOUR CUP

Caterpillar has the potential to cultivate creativity, letting go, perspective, release, restoration, surrender, and transformation.

Caterpillar affects the Kidney and Urinary Bladder meridians and the root and sacral chakras.

Contraindications: Sciatica; hamstrings; lower back issues that do not allow flexion of the spine

Instructions:

- Sit on a folded blanket or a bolster with both legs extended in front of you.
- Fold forward over the legs, allowing your back to round.
- Come to your edge (a 3 or 4 out of 10).
- Hold for five minutes.
- To come out of the pose, use your hands to push the floor away and slowly roll up.
- Lean back on your hands to release the hips and gently shake out the legs.

Modifications: Bend your knees and place a bolster underneath; rest your chest on a bolster.

Visit the Wellness Library to engage with this practice via video and audio:
https://well4edu.org/w4e/caterpillar-restorative

Spinal Twist

Figure 10.6 Spinal Twist.

FILL YOUR CUP

Spinal Twist has the potential to cultivate letting go, perspective, release, surrender, and transformation.

Spinal Twist affects the Urinary Bladder, Gall Bladder, Heart, Lung, Small Intestines, and Large Intestines meridians and the root, sacral, solar plexus, heart, and throat chakras.

Contraindications: Knee, back, or hip issues

Instructions:

- Lay on your back and pull your knees into your chest.
- Bring your arms out to your sides in a *T* position or above the head in a *Y* position.
- Exhale drop the knees over to the left side of your body, twisting the spine, and lowering the body.
- Come to your edge (a 3 or 4 out of 10).
- Stay for three to five minutes on one side.
- Once you're finished with one side, gently bring the knees into the chest and draw circles with the knees on the ceiling above to counter the twist.
- Repeat on the other side.
- Once you're finished with one side, gently bring the knees into the chest and draw circles with the knees on the ceiling above to counter the twist.

Modifications: Place a blanket under your knees to support the twist if bringing the knees to the floor is too much for the spine.

Visit the Wellness Library to engage with this practice via video and audio:
  https://well4edu.org/w4e/supine-twist

Final Relaxation

Figure 10.7 Final Relaxation.

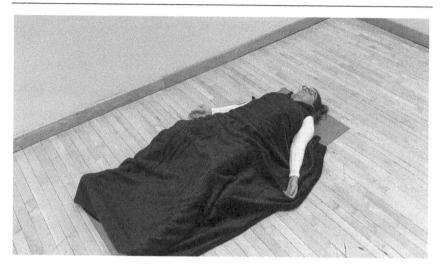

FILL YOUR CUP

Final Relaxation has the potential to cultivate letting go, openness, perspective, release, restoration, surrender, and trust.

Final Relaxation affects all the meridians and all of the chakras.

Instructions:

- Lay on your back.
- If it's comfortable for you, place a blanket, pillow, or bolster underneath the backs of the knees to alleviate tension in the lower back.
- Cover yourself with a blanket.
- Place an eye pillow or covering if it feels comfortable for you.

> Visit the Wellness Library to engage with this practice via video and audio:
> https://well4edu.org/w4e/savasana

Yin yoga has many other practices that you can learn about. We've reached the end of our practices. In the next and final chapter of the book, we emphasize the importance of not only continuing the conversation, but also acting toward systemic changes that intentionally supports educator wellbeing.

ADDITIONAL RESOURCES

If you'd like to learn more about the practice of yin yoga, I've included some resources. There are plenty more resources; these are the ones I personally recommend to others and go back to as references.

Books

Bernie Clark – *The Complete Guide to Yin Yoga: The Philosophy & Practice of Yin Yoga*
Paul Grilley – *Yin Yoga: Principles & Practice*
Biff Mithoefer – *The Yin Yoga Kit: The Practice of Quiet Power*
Dr. Hiroshi Motoyama – *Theories of the Chakras: Bridge to Higher Consciousness*
Sarah Powers – *Insight Yoga: An Innovative Synthesis of Traditional Yoga, Meditation, and Eastern Approaches to Healing and Well-Being*
Sagel Urlacher – *Yin Yoga & Meditation: A Mandala Map for Practice, Teaching, and Beyond*

Websites

Bernie Clark – https://yinyoga.com/
Sagel Urlacher – https://www.yinandmeditation.com/

CHAPTER 11

Beyond
the Band-Aids

Even though we've reached the end of this book, this is not the end of this discussion. Our work at Wellness for Educators and the work of many other organizations focuses on whole school wellness, and mental health and wellbeing. We know that this needs to be an ongoing conversation.

Just because everyone is "back to school" does not mean everyone is well and healed from the prolonged stress and trauma that has been endured even before pre-pandemic times. As Dr. Peter Levine shared, "Trauma has become so commonplace that most people don't even recognize its presence. It affects everyone. Each of us has had a traumatic experience at some point in our lives, regardless of whether it left us with an obvious case of post-traumatic stress" (p. 41). Many in our field are choosing to ignore prolonged stress and trauma.

If we ignore prolonged stress and trauma and do not take the time that is needed to heal, educators, students, parents, caregivers, and communities will continue to experience burnout, secondary traumatic stress, post-traumatic stress disorder, and more. Issues will not only resurface, but they will become more complex, and, in some ways, may be more difficult to address.

One of the school leaders we worked with during the 2022–23 school year shared the following about his own experience:

"I realized how numb I have become to trauma. I am of the opinion that everyone needs healing. The mind-body connection is not only showing me how to help others, but more importantly it shows me how to help myself."

– *School Leader*

As the ACEs Study found, "contrary to conventional belief, time does not heal all wounds since humans convert traumatic and stressful emotional experiences into organic disease." Mind-body practices, such as the ones shared in this book, can help us feel safe in our bodies again after a traumatic or stressful experience. Eventually, these practices also have the potential to lead us to feel safer in the world around us. As we feel safer, our ability to engage with others and create trusting relationships improves as well. As Dr. Cathy Cavanaugh, one of my mentors and our first board chair shares, "The ripples of our own healing can support the healing of others. Educators are helpers by nature. Sometimes motivation to care for oneself comes from the opportunity to help others."

Dr. Levine said it best when he said, "I have little doubt that as individuals, families, communities, and even nations, we have the capacity to learn how to heal and prevent much of the damage done by trauma" (Healing Trauma: A Pioneering Program for Restoring the Wisdom of Your Body). The Trauma Foundation's video conveyed, "Many of the activities that we intuitively know make us feel better – like spending time in nature, practicing yoga, dancing, helping others, and more – can help the autonomic nervous system become more regulated and resistant" (7:20).

Mind-body practices have the potential to affect change at the individual level and can reverberate when practiced at a school and community level. However, mind-body practices will do absolutely nothing when there are no intentional changes to a system that needs to be fixed. The many Band-Aids – jeans on Friday, donuts in the teachers' lounge, movie tickets, four-day work weeks (when there's no change in the amount of work that needs to be done), among many others – that are being used to create quick fixes are not going to make a difference in supporting, retaining, and recruiting educators. An intentional system-wide wellness approach that is equitable, anti-racist, and inclusive is necessary to affect meaningful change.

Educators need to be respected for the professionals they are.
Educators need tasks taken off their plates.
Educators need room to be creative.
Educators need the support of other educators so that they don't have to wear so many hats themselves.
Educators need smaller class sizes.
Educators need increased salaries.
Educators need additional support systems, such as mentoring.
Educators need more access to resources to support themselves.

Educators need more access to resources to support their students.

Educators need to be listened to.

Educators need to see their voices being heard and participate in the change that results from what they've voiced.

Educators need to be supported and protected.

Educators need to feel safe.

Educators need to have time to heal.

Educators need to have space to connect and collaborate with others.

Educators need to have space to communicate with others.

Educators need to feel like they are trusted.

Educators need to be trusted.

Educators need to feel supported.

Educators need to feel like they belong.

Educators need to be part of the conversations.

Educators need to feel valued.

There are many other things educators need that contribute to their mental health and wellbeing. In 2021, during a book study with the Council for Leaders in Alabama Schools and the Alabama State Department of Educators, we heard from several leaders about how they were feeling, and one of the educators stated what they needed so poignantly:

I wish everyone understood that educators are human beings also. We have the same struggles as everyone else and are susceptible to all that goes along with being human. We carry the weight of every child, faculty, and staff member in addition to what we carry ourselves. Kids are definitely first, but we as educators do matter and we aren't expendable.

School Leader in Alabama

As is mentioned in Chapter 1, I was driven to write this book and share it with the field of education at large because of the meaningful impact these mind-body concepts, practices, and strategies have had on my life, both personally and professionally. While this book is focused on an action plan for educators personally, I encourage you to share this book with others in your school and district. Introduce the book to your wellness committees, and if you don't have a committee, be the agent of change for your school and/or district to implement one. Taking action at the personal level is so important, and then being the lighthouse for others around you, including colleagues, students, parents, caregivers, and the system at large, is vital.

Stay tuned for three more books in this series. In the meantime, we'll continue to engage in the hard conversations to advocate for meaningful change so that educators can truly be well and feel supported and valued. We hope you do the same.

INTENTIONAL PAUSE

After reading the thoughts and ideas in this book, take a final intentional pause to reflect.

➤ What do I notice in my mind? (observe without judgment)
➤ What do I notice in my body? (observe without judgment)
➤ What do I notice in my feelings? (observe without judgment)
➤ What do I notice in my thoughts? (observe without judgment)
➤ What do I need at this moment to feel supported? (observe without judgment and give yourself what you need to feel supported)

REFERENCES

Abbott, R., and Lavretsky, H. (2013). Tai chi and Qigong for the treatment and prevention of mental disorders. *Psychiatric Clinics of North America* 36: 109–110. doi:10.1016/j.psc.2013.01.011.

Akiba, M., Chiu, Y., Shimizu, K., et al. (2012). Teacher salary and national achievement: A cross-national analysis of 30 countries. *International Journal of Educational Research* 53: 171–181. doi:10.1016/j.ijer.2012.03.007.

Allensworth, D.D., and Kolbe, L.J. (1987). The comprehensive school health program: Exploring an expanded concept. *Journal of School Health* 57: 409–412.

Amin, A., et al. (2016). Beneficial effects of OM chanting on depression, anxiety, stress and cognition in elderly women with hypertension. *Indian Journal of Clinical Anatomy and Physiology* 3 (3): 253–255.

Anheyer D., Klose P., Lauche R., et al. (2020). Yoga for treating headaches: A systematic review and meta-analysis. *Journal of General Internal Medicine.* 35 (3): 846–854.

Bakker, A.B., Hakanen, J.J., Demerouti, E., et al. (2007). Job resources boost work engagement, particularly when job demands are high. *Journal of Educational Psychology* 99 (2): 274–284. doi:10.1037/0022-0663.99.2.274.

Ball, S. (2003). The teacher's soul and the terrors of performativity. *Journal of Education Policy* 18 (2): 215–228. doi:10.1080/0268093022000043065.

Borman, G., and Dowling, N. (2008). Teacher attrition and retention: A meta-analytic and narrative review of the research. *Review of Educational Research* 78 (3): 367–409. doi:10.3102/0034654308321455.

Britton, J., and Propper, C. (2016). Teacher pay and school productivity: Exploiting wage regulation. *Journal of Public Economics* 133: 75–89. doi:10.1016/j.jpubeco.2015.12.004.

Buckley, J. (2004). The Effects of School Facility Quality on Teacher Retention in Urban School Districts. National Institute of Building Sciences – National Clearinghouse for Educational Facilities.

Bullock, G. (2019). What focusing on the breath does to your brain. *Greater Good Magazine* (31 October).

Butzer, B., and Flynn, L. (2018). Seven ways that yoga is good for schools. *Greater Good Magazine* (20 November).

Carver-Thomas, D., and Darling-Hammond, L. (2017). Teacher turnover: Why it matters and what we can do about it. Learning Policy Institute, Palo Alto, CA.

Cazes, S., Hijzen, A., and Saint-Martin, A. (2015). Measuring and assessing job quality: The OECD Job Quality Framework. OECD Social, Employment and Migration Working Papers, No. 174, OECD Publishing, Paris. doi:10.1787/5jrp02kjw1mr-en.

Centers for Disease Control and Prevention. (2012). Parent engagement: Strategies for involving parents in school health. Atlanta, GA: US Department of Health and Human Services.

Chan, J.S.M., Ho, R.T.H., Wang, C.W., et al. (2013). Effects of qigong exercise on fatigue, anxiety, and depressive symptoms of patients with chronic fatigue syndrome-like illness: A randomized controlled trial. *Evidence-Based Complementary and Alternative Medicine* 2013: 485341. doi:10.1155/2013/485341.

Clark, B. (2012). *The Complete Guide to Yin Yoga: The Philosophy and Practice of Yin Yoga*. Texas: Wild Strawberry Productions.

Cochran-Smith, M. (2004). Stayers, leavers, lovers, and dreamers. *Journal of Teacher Education* 55 (5): 387–392. doi:10.1177/0022487104270188.

Cohen, D., Boudhar, S., Bowler, A., et al. (2016). Blood pressure effects of yoga, alone or in combination with lifestyle measures: Results of the Lifestyle Modification and Blood Pressure Study (LIMBS). *The Journal of Clinical Hypertension* 18 (8): 809–816.

Collie, R., Shapka, J., and Perry, N. (2012). School climate and social-emotional learning: Predicting teacher stress, job satisfaction, and teaching efficacy. *Journal of Educational Psychology* 104 (4): 1189–1204. doi:10.1037/a0029356.

Collie, R., Shapka, J., and Perry, N. (2015). Teacher well-being: Exploring its components and a practice-oriented scale. *Journal of Psychoeducational Assessment* 33 (8): 744–756. doi:10.1177/0734282915587990.

Craig, C. (2017). International teacher attrition: Multiperspective views. *Teachers and Teaching* 23 (8): 859–862. doi:10.1080/13540602.2017.1360860.

Cregg, D.R., and Cheavens, J.S. (2021). Gratitude interventions: Effective self-help? A meta-analysis of the impact on symptoms of depression and anxiety. *Journal of Happiness Studies* 22, 413–445. doi:10.1007/s10902-020-00236-6.

Dechar, L.E. (2006). *Five Spirits: Alchemical Acupuncture for Psychological and Spiritual Healing*. New York: Lantern Publishing & Media.

Diener, E. (2006). Guidelines for national indicators of subjective well-being and ill-being. *Applied Research in Quality of Life* 1/2: 151–157. doi:10.1007/s11482-006-9007-x.

Earthman, G.I., and Lemasters, L.K. (2009). Teacher attitudes about classroom conditions. *Journal of Educational Administration* 47 (3), 323–335.

Felitti, V.J., Anda, R.F., Nordenberg, D., et al. (1998). Relationship of childhood abuse and household dysfunction to many of the leading causes of death in adults. The Adverse Childhood Experiences (ACE) Study. *American Journal of Preventive Medicine* 14 (4): 245–258.

Franks, L.J. (2016). *Stone Medicine: A Chinese Medicine Guide to Healing With Gems and Minerals.* Rochester, VT: Healing Arts Press.

GENYOUth Foundation. (2014). GENYOUth Foundation Progress Report 2014: The Quest for Healthy, High-Achieving Schools. Retrieved from https://genyouthnow.org/wp-content/uploads/2020/11/Progress Report.pdf.

Gerritsen, R.J.S., and Band, G.P.H. (2018). Breath of life: The respiratory vagal stimulation model of contemplative activity. *Frontiers in Human Neuroscience* 12: 397.

Gray, L., and Taie, S. (2015). Public school teacher attrition and mobility in the first five years: Results from the first through fifth waves of the 2007–08 Beginning Teacher Longitudinal Study. U.S. Department of Education. Washington, D.C.: National Center for Education Statistics.

Grilley, P. (2012). *Yin Yoga: Principles & Practice.* Ashland, OR: White Cloud Press.

Grodin, M. A., Piwowarczyk, L., Fulker, D., et al. (2008). Treating survivors of torture and refugee trauma: A preliminary case series using Qigong and t'ai chi. *Journal of Alternative and Complementary Medicine* 14: 801–806. doi:10.1089/acm.2007.0736.

Gunaratana, H. (2012). *The Foundations of Mindfulness in Plain English.* Somerville, MA: Wisdom Publications.

Gunaratana, H. (n.d.). What exactly is Vipassana meditation? Tricycle: *The Buddhist Review.* Retrieved from https://tricycle.org/magazine/vipassana-meditation/.

Hagins, M., and Rundle, A. (2016). Yoga improves academic performance in urban high school students compared to physical education: A randomized controlled trial. *Mind, Brain, and Education* 10 (2).

Hakanen, J., Bakker, A., and Schaufeli, W. (2006). Burnout and work engagement among teachers. *Journal of School Psychology* 43 (6): 495–513. doi:10.1016/j.jsp.2005.11.001.

Halliwell, E. (2018). Can meditation help you with depression? *Greater Good Magazine* (5 October).

Halpern, C. (2010). Quiet justice. *Greater Good Magazine* (29 June).

Hargreaves, A. (2003). *Teaching in the Knowledge Society: Education in the Age of Insecurity*. New York: Teachers College Press.

Harris, A.R., Jennings, P.A., Katz, D.A., Abenavoli, R.M., and Greenberg, M.T. (2016). Promoting stress management and well-being in educators: Outcomes of the CALM intervention. *Mindfulness* 7: 143–154.

Hendricks, M. (2015). Towards an optimal teacher salary schedule: Designing base salary to attract and retain effective teachers. *Economics of Education Review* 47: 143–167. doi:10.1016/j.econedurev.2015.05.008.

Hendricks, M. (2014). Does it pay to pay teachers more? Evidence from Texas. *Journal of Public Economics* 109: 50–63. doi:10.1016/j.jpubeco.2013.11.001.

Ingersoll, R. (2003). Is there really a teacher shortage? *University of Pennsylvania ScholarlyCommons*.

Jahnke, R., Larkey, L., Rogers, C., et al. (2010). A comprehensive review of health benefits of Qigong and tai chi. *American Journal of Health Promotion* 24 (6): e1–e25. doi:10.4278/ajhp.081013-LIT-248.

Johns Hopkins Medicine: Health. (n.d.). Muscle pain: It may actually be your fascia. Retrieved from https://www.hopkinsmedicine.org/health/wellness-and-prevention/muscle-pain-it-may-actually-be-your-fascia.

Jotkoff, E. (2022). NEA survey: Massive staff shortages in schools leading to educator burnout: alarming number of educators indicating they plan to leave profession.

Kabat-Zinn, J. (2003). Mindfulness-based interventions in context: past, present, and future. *Clinical Psychology: Science and Practice* 10: 144–156.

Kaptchuk, T.J. (2000). *The Web That Has No Weaver: Understanding Chinese Medicine*. New York: Contemporary Books.

Kim, S.H., Schneider, S.M., Kravitz, L., Mermier, C., et al. (2013). Mind-body practices for posttraumatic stress disorder. *Journal of Investigative Medicine* 61: 827–834. doi:10.231/JIM.0b013e3182906862.

Kinnunen, U., and Salo, K. (1994). Teacher stress: An eight-year follow-up study on teachers' work, stress, and health. *Anxiety, Stress, & Coping* 7 (4): 319–337. doi:10.1080/10615809408249355.

Klassen, R., Foster, R., Rajani, S., et al. (2009). Teaching in the Yukon: Exploring teachers' efficacy beliefs, stress, and job satisfaction in a remote setting. *International Journal of Educational Research* 48 (6): 381–394. doi:10.1016/j.ijer.2010.04.002.

Kolbe, L. (2002). Education reform and the goals of modern school health programs. *The State Education Standard* 3 (4): 4–11.

Lee, M.S., Kang, C.W., Lim, H.J., et al. (2004a). Effects of Qi-training on anxiety and plasma concentrations of cortisol, ACTH, and aldosteroneAa randomized placebo-controlled pilot study. *Stress Health* 20: 243–248. doi:10.1002/smi.1023.

Lee, M.S., Rim, Y.H., and Kang, C.W. (2004b). Effects of external Qi-therapy on emotions, electroencephalograms, and plasma cortisol. *International Journal of Neuroscience* 114: 1493–1502. doi:10.1080/00207450490509113.

Levine, P. (1997). *Waking the Tiger: Healing Trauma*. Berkeley, CA: North Atlantic Books.

Li, G., Yuan, H., and Zhang, W. (2014). Effects of Tai Chi on health related quality of life in patients with chronic conditions: A systematic review of randomized controlled trials. *Complementary Therapies in Medicine* 22: 743–55.

Li, Y., Li, S., Jiang, J., et al. (2019). Effects of yoga on patients with chronic nonspecific neck pain: A PRISMA systematic review and meta-analysis. *Medicine (Baltimore)* 98 (8): e14649.

Liu, X., Clark, J., Siskind, D., et al. (2015). A systematic review and meta-analysis of the effects of Qigong and Tai Chi for depressive symptoms. *Complementary Therapies in Medicine* 23: 516–534. doi:10.1016/j.ctim.2015.05.001.

McCallum, F., and Price, D. (2010). Well teachers, well students. *The Journal of Student Wellbeing* 4 (1): 19. doi:10.21913/jsw.v4i1.599.

McCallum, F., Price, D., Graham, A., et al. (2017). Teacher Wellbeing: A review of the literature. Association of Independent Schools of NSW, Sydney.

Martinez, N., Martorelli, C., Espinosa, L., et al. (2015). Impact of Qigong on quality of life, pain and depressive symptoms in older adults admitted to an intermediate care rehabilitation unit: A randomized controlled trial. *Aging Clinical and Experimental Research* 27: 125–130. doi:10.1007/s40520-014-0250-y.

Mindful (2016). Jon Kabat-Zinn: Defining mindfulness. https://www.mindful .org/jon-kabat-zinn-defining-mindfulness/ (accessed 27 June 2022).

Mithoefer, B. (2006). *The Yin Yoga Kit: The Practices of Quiet Power.* New York: Healing Arts Press.

Motoyama, H. (2018). *Theories of the Chakras: Bridge to Higher Consciousness.* New Delhi, India: New Age Books.

Monson, A., Chismark, A., Cooper, B. et al. (2017). Effects of yoga on musculoskeletal pain. *Journal of Dental Hygiene* 91 (2): 15–22.

Moore Johnson, S.M. (2012). How context matters in high-need schools: The effects of teachers' working conditions on their professional satisfaction and their students' achievement. *Teachers College Record* 114 (10): 1–39.

Mostafa, T., and Pál, J. (2018). Science teachers' satisfaction: Evidence from the PISA 2015 teacher survey. OECD Education Working Papers, No. 168, OECD Publishing, Paris. doi:10.1787/1ecdb4e3-en.

Newman, K.M. (2020). Is the way you breathe making you anxious? *Greater Good Magazine.* (10 November).

Nordqvist, J. (2021). What are the health benefits of tai chi? *Medical News Today* (6 April).

OECD. (2019). TALIS 2018 Results (Volume I): Teachers and School Leaders as Lifelong Learners, TALIS. *OECD Publishing,* Paris. doi:10.1787/1d0bc92a-en.

OECD. (2014). TALIS 2013 Results: An International Perspective on Teaching and Learning, TALIS. *OECD Publishing,* Paris. doi:10.1787/9789264196261-en.

OECD. (2013). How's Life? 2013: Measuring Well-being. *OECD Publishing*, Paris. doi:10.1787/9789264201392-en.

Pandi-Perumal, S.R., Spence, D.W., Srivastava, N., et al. (2022). The origin and clinical relevance of yoga nidra. *Sleep Vigilance* 6: 61–84. doi:10.1007/s41782-022-00202-7.

Porges, S.W. (2011). *The Polyvagal Theory: Neurophysiological Foundations of Emotions, Attachment, Communication, and Self-regulation*. New York: W.W. Norton.

Powers, S. (2008). *Insight Yoga: An Innovative Synthesis of Traditional Yoga, Meditation, and Eastern Approaches to Healing and Well-Being*. Boulder, CO: Shambhala.

Qaseem, A., Wilt, T.J., McLean, R.M., et al. (2017). Noninvasive treatments for acute, subacute, and chronic low back pain: A clinical practice guideline from the American College of Physicians. *Annals of Internal Medicine* 166 (7): 514–530.

Rajkumar, L., Dubowy, C., and Khatib, A. (2021). Impact of practicing mindful breathing in class. *Teaching and Learning Excellence through Scholarship*, 1(1). doi:10.52938/tales.v1i1.1361.

Rosenkranz, M.A., Davidson, R.J., Maccoon, D.G., et al. (2013). A comparison of mindfulness-based stress reduction and an active control in modulation of neurogenic inflammation. *Brain, behavior, and immunity* 27: 174–184. doi:10.1016/j.bbi.2012.10.013.

Ross, C.E., and Wu C. (1995). The links between education and health. *American Sociological Review* 60 (5): 719–745.

Schleicher, A. (2018). Valuing our Teachers and Raising their Status: How Communities Can Help, International Summit on the Teaching Profession. *OECD Publishing, Paris*. doi:10.1787/9789264292697-en.

Shinnick, P. (2006). Qigong: Where did it come from? Where does it fit in science? What are the advances? *Journal of Alternative & Complementary Medicine* 12: 351–353. doi:10.1089/acm.2006.12.351.

Siegel, D. (2008). *The neurobiology of "we": How relationships, the mind, and the brain interact to shape who we are*. UCLA Mindful Awareness Research Center.

Siegel, D. (1999). *The Developing Mind: Toward a Neurobiology of Interpersonal Experience*. New York, NY: Guilford Publications.

Simon-Thomas, E.R. (2013). Meditation makes us act with compassion. *Greater Good Magazine*. (11 April).

Steiner, E. D., Doan, S., Woo, A., et al. (2022). Restoring teacher and principal well-being is an essential step for rebuilding schools: Findings from the State of the American Teacher and State of the American Principal Surveys. Santa Monica, CA: RAND Corporation.

Stenlund, T., Ahlgren, C., Lindahl, B., et al. (2009). Cognitively oriented behavioral rehabilitation in combination with Qigong for patients on long-term sick leave because of burnout: REST – A randomized clinical trial. *International Journal of Behavioral Medicine* 16: 294–303. doi:10.1007/s12529-008-9011-7.

Stenlund, T., Nordin, M., and Järvholm, L.S. (2012). Effects of rehabilitation programmes for patients on long-term sick leave for burnout: A 3-year follow-up of the rest study. *Journal of Rehabilitation Medicine* 44: 684–690. doi:10.2340/16501977-1003.

Sun, Y. (1988). The influence of Qigong and Taijiquan in respiratory rehabilitation. *Chinese Journal of Rehabilitation Medicine* 4: 168.

Suttie, J. (2018). Five ways mindfulness meditation is good for your health. *Greater Good Magazine*. (24 October).

Tsang, H.W.H., Cheung, L, and Lak, D.C.C. (2002). Qigong as a psychosocial intervention for depressed elderly with chronic physical illness. *International Journal of Geriatric Psychiatry* 17: 1146–1154. doi:10.1002/gps.739.

Tsang, H.W., Mok, C.K., Au Yeung, Y.T., et al. (2003). The effect of Qigong on general and psychological health of elderly with chronic physical illnesses. A randomized clinical trial. *International Journal of Geriatric Psychiatry* 18: 441–449. doi:10.1002/gps.861.

UIS. (2016). The world needs almost 69 million new teachers to reach the 2030 Education goals. UIS fact sheet, Vol. 39.

Urlacher, S. (2022). *Yin Yoga & Meditation: A Mandala Map for Practice, Teaching, and Beyond*. Tucson, AZ: Sacred Nature Press.

U.S. Department of Education, Office of Planning, Evaluation and Policy Development, Policy and Program Studies Service (2016). The state of racial diversity in the educator workforce. Washington, D.C.

Valosek, L., Wendt, S., Link, J., et al. (2021). Meditation effective in reducing teacher burnout and improving resilience: A randomized controlled study. *Frontiers in Education* 6. doi:10.3389/feduc.2021.627923.

van der Kolk, B. (2014). *The Body Keeps the Score: Brain, Mind, and Body in the Healing of Trauma.* New York: Viking Press.

van Horn, J.E., Taris, T.W., Schaufeli, W.B. et al. (2010). The structure of occupational well-being: A study among Dutch teachers. *Journal of Occupational and Organizational Psychology* 77 (3): 365–375.

Viac, C., and Fraser, P. (2020, Jan). Teachers' well-being: A framework for data collection and analysis. OECD Education Working Paper No. 213.

Villemure, C., Ceko, M., Cotton, V.A., et al. (2015). Neuroprotective effects of yoga practice: Age-, experience-, and frequency-dependent plasticity. *Frontiers in Human Neuroscience* 9. doi:10.3389/fnhum.2015.00281.

Wang, C.W., Chan, C.L., Ho, R.T., et al. (2013). The effect of Qigong on depressive and anxiety symptoms: a systematic review and meta-analysis of randomized controlled trials. *Evidence-Based Complementary and Alternative Medicine* 2013: 716094. doi:10.1155/2013/716094.

Wang, F., Man, J.K.M., Lee, E.-K. O., et al. (2013). The effects of Qigong on anxiety, depression, and psychological well-being: a systematic review and meta-analysis. *Evidence-Based Complementary and Alternative Medicine* 2013:152738. doi:10.1155/2013/152738.

Wang, W. (2016). Chapter 15 – Genomics and Traditional Chinese Medicine. *ScienceDirect,* 293–309.

Watkins, P.C., Woodward, K., Stone, T., et al. (2003). Gratitude and happiness: Development of a measure of gratitude, and relationships with subjective well-being. *Social Behavior and Personality: An international journal* 31 (5): 431–451. doi:10.2224/sbp.2003.31.5.431.

Wayne, P.M., and Fuerst, M.L. (2013). *The Harvard Medical School guide to tai chi: 12 weeks to a healthy body, strong heart and sharp mind.* Colorado: Shambhala Publications.

Yang, J.-M. (1989). *The Root of Chinese Qigong: Secrets for Health, Longevity, and Enlightenment.* Wolfeboro, NH: YMAA Publication Center.

Yeung, A., Slipp, L.E., Jacquart, J., et al. (2013). The treatment of depressed Chinese Americans using Qigong in a health care setting: a pilot study. *Evidence-Based Complementary and Alternative Medicine* 2013:168784. doi:10.3390/ijerph110909186.

Yin, J., and Dishman, R.K. (2014). The effect of Tai Chi and Qigong practice on depression and anxiety symptoms: A systematic review and meta-regression analysis of randomized controlled trials. *Mental Health and Physical Activity* 7: 135–146. doi:10.1016/j.mhpa.2014.08.001.

Zheng, J., and Keltner, D. (2020). Why yoga is good for your body and brain, according to science. *Greater Good Magazine* (24 August).

INDEX

Page numbers followed by *f* refer to figures.